BEING HUMAN

Essays on Thoughtmares, Bouncing Back, and Your True Nature

AMY JOHNSON PH.D.

For Willow and Miller, obviously.

PERMISSIONS

My intention for this work is that it is widely shared with
as many people as possible. Please feel free to reprint,
publish, and share any part of this book with anyone who
you think might benefit from it. If you do, please include the
following with any portion you reprint:

Reprinted by permission of the author,
Dr. Amy Johnson (www.DrAmyJohnson.com).

Interior and Cover Art by Janette Gregson
(http://ajsartjournal.wordpress.com/)
Cover Design by Shea McGuire
(www.OnaBudgetDesign.com)
Edited by Lynn Hess (www.PremierProofing.com)

CONTENTS

"Do you know what happens to wildlife when left alone from intellectual minds? It thrives, because thriving is its default setting. Just look at a forest.

And do you know what happens to wildlife when given just a little direction by intellectual minds? It still thrives, because thriving is its default setting. Just look at a rose garden.

And do you know what happens to wildlife when there is too much thinking? Yeah, what wildlife?

Wild thing,

The Universe"

—The Universe (via Mike Dooley, www.tut.com)

Introduction

I was relaxing in my living room in Michigan on a humid afternoon in the summer of 2012, laptop on lap, ear buds in ears, listening to a talk from the 2011 Innate Health Conference held in London 6 months earlier.

The speaker said something that blew my mind. It was incredibly simple and delivered with no emphasis or fanfare whatsoever.

He said that the default, innate nature of all human beings is wellbeing.

That we are all perfectly mentally healthy, full of the clarity and peace of mind we so often chase. He said wellness is our birthright and can't possibly be erased; he also said that when we're not feeling connected to our innate wellness it's only because our personal thinking is in the way, clouding that natural connection.

I backed up the audio and listened five or ten more times to be sure I was hearing him correctly. And then I did something that was very uncharacteristic of me: I pulled out the ear buds, closed the laptop, and lay down on the couch.

While I would typically hear something that resonated with me and want more, more, more, comparing what I had just heard with everything else I had ever learned (How was this like that other theory? How does this fit with what so-and-so has to say? What can I read or Google or who can I call to learn more?) I didn't feel like I wanted more this time. Not in that moment. I wanted to lie in silence for a bit and soak it all in.

In hindsight, what I heard the speaker say on that hot July afternoon shouldn't have shocked me in the least. Besides the fact that I was tuned into a conference called Innate Health (What did I *think* they'd be talking about?), I already knew this stuff.

I had been studying spirituality—along with psychology, mythology, philosophy, and more mainstream self-help—since I was an angst-filled teenager 20 years ago. I was a master certified life coach with a doctorate degree in psychology. I had been working with clients, essentially teaching them that they are inherently well, for nearly a decade.

I already knew that we are all fundamentally connected to each other and to something supremely benevolent that powers all of life.

I was already wholly on board with the idea that we are all born with a direct connection to that universal force. Even as we grow up and feel like the connection has faded, it hasn't. Because it's *who we are*, it can't fade.

And I was already well aware that taking your own idle thinking at face value was the primary cause of suffering.

So why was I so blown away that summer day? It was partly the conviction with which the speaker stated these facts; although I can't remember his name I vividly recall his confidence.

But mostly, it was the simplicity of it all. You are well, period. Everyone on earth. Essentially. Always.

There are no exceptions, caveats, conditions, or rules to remember and there is absolutely nothing you have to do—nothing you even *can* do—to make it more or less true.

Are you skeptical? If you are noticing that in this very moment you are most certainly *not* in touch with your innate wellbeing, I hear you. But ask yourself this: If wellbeing and peace of mind are not home base, why do you fight so hard to return there when you're not there? If stress and mental chaos were home base they would feel like home, wouldn't they? They might feel unpleasant, but they would be natural, familiar, and comfortable on some level.

Stress and mental busyness go against your nature and that's why you struggle to "fix" them. That's why you scramble to return home, to the wellness into which you were born.

Rather than assuming that you have no innate wellbeing, consider instead that you might simply be experiencing a whole mess of personal thinking which appears to cloud your perfect, natural state.

When you're not experiencing your emotional wellness it's only because you are caught up in otherwise arbitrary and habitual thought. Those moments of supreme peace you sometimes experience are *who you naturally are.* When you're experiencing anything else, you're simply in a fog of thought.

Nothing can change your basic nature. Not age, culture, or conditioning. Not abuse, a horrible childhood, or totally unfit parents.

Not joblessness, homelessness, or a truly horrific break-up. Not depression, anxiety, or schizophrenia. Not fear, worry, or obsession.

Your innate wellbeing goes nowhere—it's always right there, only sometimes masked by mental chit-chat.

Isn't that just about the best news you've ever heard?

WHAT THIS MEANS FOR YOU

Something truly magical happens when you deeply get that the thoughts that roll through your mind all day long are not *yours.* You aren't the thinker of your thoughts, any more than you are the breather of your lungs or the beater of your heart.

It's much more accurate to say that thought arises within you than to say that *you* think it, like it's more accurate to say that breath arises within you than to say that *you* have to breathe your breath.

Universal energy takes care of generating thought. It's not your job. If you don't hold your breath, new breath rushes in. Similarly, if you don't "hold" your thoughts (attach to, identify with them), new thought rushes in. There's nothing you have to do.

You are an open channel through which inner wisdom—that inexplicably wise guidance to which we all have access—can and does pass. The only thing that ever temporarily blocks that open channel is personal thinking.

Personal thinking is that inner dialogue that is yours and yours alone. It's your own brand of highly subjective, often biased, sometimes habitual mental chit-chat.

It's that voice in your head that already knows what your partner will say even before you ask a question; the one that has warned you that you'll probably end up alone, or played out the same fantasy of winning the lottery, or convinced you that ice cream makes everything better for as long as you can remember. Personal thinking is not always harmful, heavy, or habitual—the innocent, random, fleeting thought you experience is personal thinking as well. Personal thinking is essentially the mental dialogue that is always running in your head and that makes up your experience of life.

The good news about personal thinking is that it is always moving. The nature of thought is to flow and constantly change and it will always do that when you don't interfere. You interfere when you attach to or identify with thought as if it's "yours"—part of who you are.

If you doubt that thought is insignificant and effortlessly arising within you, watch a two year old. She doesn't identify with or attach to thought, and so her thoughts and emotions flow freely and quickly, un-messed with.

(And if you doubt that your true nature is peace of mind and well-being, keep watching that two year old. She may have all kinds of fast-moving thoughts and emotions on the surface—even those that produce fits and tantrums—but because nothing sticks for long, she's constantly bounced right back into her natural wellbeing.)

In addition to always moving and changing, thoughts are also habitual (you have most of the same thoughts today as you did yesterday), subjective (your thoughts are exclusive to you, based on your own unique view of the world), and *completely meaningless* in and of themselves.

One hundred percent of your experience of life comes from thought. Your experience of life is internally generated from within you—inside-out. Quite inconveniently, life always appears as if it's outside-in; as if things outside of you directly impact your experience. They do not. Your consciousness brings your thinking to life like a film projector brings the images on the film to life, resulting in your unique, thought-based reality.

If you're like most people, it can be very difficult to buy into the notion that outside events and other people do not directly impact how you feel. The truth of the matter is that your entire experience of life—including all of your emotions, reactions, and feelings—are created from within you, via thought.

Our perceptual system is designed such that it truly appears as if outside events directly affect us. It looks like being snubbed by your date creates your embarrassment and shame. It really feels like your home flooding or your dog getting sick or your spouse's incessant complaining is creating your frustration and pain. And yet, it's always your *thinking about those things* that creates your experience, not the circumstances themselves.

No two people would react to those events in the exact same way because no two people have the exact same thinking. Even you wouldn't react to those events in the same way at different points in time. We live an entirely thought-created experience even when—no, *especially* when—it seems as if we don't. When it looks *most compelling* that your hellish boss or the lack of money in your account is creating your emotional state, that's exactly when you have the most personal thinking at play.

Wild, isn't it? Wild, and also incredibly freeing. This is Being Human.

THERE IS NOTHING TO DO

Given that your true nature is endless wellbeing, clarity, and peace of mind...and given that new thought is always showing up for you when you don't interfere with the process by holding on to old thought...there's simply nothing to do but *understand the way the system works.*

When you have a deep appreciation for how your experience really works, you can rest in that understanding. When you get just how naturally you are constantly being bounced back to your natural state of clarity and peace, the endless trying and striving and working toward things that you think will make you feel better falls away. There is simply no need to *do* so much. Doing never delivers the feelings you expect it to, anyway.

You can't think yourself back to clarity and you don't have to. You *are* clarity, occasionally covered with thought to which you are clinging. A return to your clear nature only requires that you withdraw your effort and energy, and wait.

When you insightfully get that your entire experience of life is thought-created and that thought is impermanent and meaningless, there's nothing more to do.

YOU MIGHT HATE ME A LITTLE BIT

As I suggest throughout this book that life is so much easier than you're making it, and that there is really nothing to do; that you can stop the striving because you're already "there," already perfect, and already have peace of mind just under the surface, you might hate me just a little bit. If you are anything like I was not all that long ago, people who tell you to *do less* when you're very conditioned to do *more, more, more* will drive you insane.

I realize that my repeated insistence that you have endless wellbeing *now*, especially when you don't *feel* that endless wellbeing, may be annoying. I'm okay with that. I mean, I want you to enjoy reading this book and I'd rather you didn't curse me as you read it, but if that's what has to happen, I'm okay with it. Lying to you isn't an option.

Giving you the "5 Steps to Happiness," a bunch of exercises to complete in your journal before you move on to the next chapter, or daily practices and techniques isn't an option either. Peace of mind is *way* easier than all of that. When people tell me I'm taking a risk by not giving you the self-help format you're used to, I say I'll gladly take that risk. I'm not willing to make it harder than it is for the sake of handing you a book that feels familiar.

Besides, homework isn't my style. I'd rather you read for fun and allow these insights to land as they will and when they will than imagine you sitting there with a notebook and highlighter, muscling through it.

If you can read this book the way you'd read a text message from your best friend or the way you'd listen to your favorite song...easily, not analyzing the ideas as much as getting the overall *feel* of them, you'll be in a great position to get the most out of what's here.

And if my insistence that you are much closer to your infinite wellbeing than you think and that there's nothing you have to do but see it becomes annoying, I'm sorry. It's for your own good, I promise.

MORE ON INSIGHTFULLY "GETTING IT"

Like my experience listening to that Innate Health speaker last summer, you may already know much of what you read here. But there is an enormous difference between intellectually understanding something and truly getting it as a personal truth.

I can't tell you how often I hear things like, "I know that the approval of others doesn't mean I'm more worthy, but I keep chasing it anyway," or "Oh, I totally get what you're saying about our experience of life coming from within us rather than from outside events, but I'll be so much happier when I'm in the new house (job, marriage, dress size, etc.)."

If that sounds like you, you're in good company. You do "get it" to a degree, but perhaps not on the level at which I hope for you to get it. You have an intellectual understanding, but not an insightful understanding. How do you know when you've moved from a limited and relatively shallow intellectual understanding to a deep and profound insight about something? You know because your life changes. *You* don't change your life; your life simply changes.

My favorite story about the power of insight comes from author and spiritual teacher Byron Katie. In her book *I Need Your Love—Is that True?*, Katie tells of how she was once hiking in the Mojave Dessert and came face to face with a rattlesnake. She was terrified, and had thoughts like "This is the end of me" and "They'll find my body here someday"; she had physical reactions such as a racing heart, nausea, and sweaty palms; and she experienced panic and going into the fight or flight response. Then something caused Katie to look again. As she looked more closely she realized that the rattlesnake was actually a rope. As soon as she really saw that, everything changed; the scary thoughts, physical reactions, and panic vanished.

Katie says: "What had happened? I knew one thing: I was safe. I knew that I could stand over that rope for a thousand years and never be frightened of it again. I felt such gratitude and ease. The entire world could come upon this snake, scream, run away, have heart attacks, scare themselves to death—and I could just remain here fearlessly, and pass on the good news. I would understand people's fears, see their pain, hear their stories about why it really is a snake, and yet there would be no way that I could believe them or be frightened of that rope. I had fallen into the simple truth: *That snake is a rope.*"[1]

One brand new thought ("That snake is a rope") changed everything. With her new thought came a new reality, and she couldn't possibly bring herself to go back to being afraid of the rope again despite the strength of that initial fear. Katie's deep insight about the rattlesnake gave her a new truth, much like when you wake from sleep to realize that you were only dreaming, or when you show your toddler that the scary monster under the bed is only the witless cat. It's the same when you have a personal insight (i.e., a new thought) that leads you to see that what you previously took as truth is not.

---

1 Byron Katie, *I Need Your Love—Is That True? How to Stop Seeking Love, Approval, and Appreciation and Start Finding Them Instead* (New York: Three Rivers Press/ Crown Publishing Group, 2005).

As you read the essays in this book, feel for what resonates with you without thinking too much—which is great practice, anyway. The way I'm suggesting you absorb this book is actually what this book is *about*, in a sense. See if you can allow personal thought to do what it does in the background. When reasoning, analysis, and "How is this concept like that?" and "I wonder what she means by this?" take a backseat, a deeper feeling can step up and speak to you directly. That deeper feeling will often be a brand new thought—and just one brand new thought is all that's ever needed to see everything in a different light.

POST (MODERN) ENLIGHTENMENT

As you might expect, my understanding of our human experience has evolved a bit since I wrote my first book, *Modern Enlightenment: Psychological, Spiritual, and Practical Ideas for a Better Life.*

Being enlightened is remarkably simpler than I once believed.

I used to suggest you get your hands dirty in the *content* of your thinking. I'd teach you to notice and monitor your inner dialogue enough to identify the thoughts you assumed were responsible for your suffering. You could then examine, question, and analyze those thoughts.

I helped my clients apply logic to their painful thoughts in order to see them in a new way. Sometimes those thoughts would be altered as a result of all of that work; sometimes they wouldn't.

It was a very active process. And although I still consider thought content at times, as you can tell by what you've read thus far, it's more work than you need to do.

Also, while many books that may appear similar to this one espouse positive thinking, the approach here is different.

Because you're always feeling your thinking, yes, positive thoughts will certainly lead you to feel more positive than negative thoughts. To the extent that you *can* choose your thoughts, know that choosing happier ones will probably make you happier than choosing unhappy ones.

It's just that, in my experience, I'm not sure you can always choose your thoughts so easily. Thoughts arise within us and, while we do have some say in which ones we attach to and identify with, that process often happens automatically, beyond our awareness.

I don't know about you, but I've often had the experience of a thought feeling like it has such a hold on me that I couldn't change it if I tried; in fact, trying to change it puts so much attention on it that it often seems to cement the thought in place—just the opposite of what you want!

Trying to "think better thoughts," in addition to being difficult and often making your *unwanted* thoughts even stickier, can sometimes feel like a lie. It's a tough job when it works at all.

The alternative to that very active and effortful monitoring, tracking, and analyzing is this: *Understanding that thought is the source of your entire experience of life.*

When you get that *all* experience is thought-created—that what you're feeling is always and only your own thinking, not some objective reality outside of yourself—everything changes. There is no need to dissect each painful thought when you truly see that thought is arbitrary and fleeting. All you have to do is not attach to every bit of mental chit-chat that floats through your mind and wait as it's replaced with new and different chit-chat.

All you have to do is not be afraid of your own experiences and not take it all so seriously.

Although I can't imagine it getting much simpler than this, I could be wrong. With any luck, I'll continue to deepen my understanding—and, in my next book, I'll be able to point out how it's even simpler than the way it appears today.

THE THREE PRINCIPLES

Many of the ideas and observations you'll read about in this book are quite consistent with what those unusually peaceful people at the Innate Health Conference speak about, a field of Psychology also sometimes known as Psychology of Mind or The Three Principles. If you want to learn more about The Three Principles, please refer to the Resources listed at the end of this book.

Although I've been very influenced by The Principles in the past year, I don't officially write or work with clients from that perspective. What you'll read in this book is simply my current understanding of the way life works based on the entirety of the influences in my life, not least of all my own inner guidance. I've found that when I set down the thousands of books I've read and step away from the formal training and mentoring, that guidance often shows up and does much of the heavy lifting for me.

BEING HUMAN IS NOT A SELF-HELP BOOK

That's right, it's not.

You don't need to change. You certainly don't need to become a better or different version of yourself.

The cause of any "problem" you experience is the belief that things should be different than they are. The cause of any "problem" with yourself is the belief that you are lacking or need something you don't already possess. Or, as Robert Holden says, "The fear that something is wrong with you is your greatest block to joy. In truth, there is no other block."

The only "self-help" I have to offer is pointing you toward the truth about your "self" and helping you gain a deeper understanding about the human experience. Those are what this book aims to provide.

I couldn't possibly know more about how you should live your life than you do. This book is not a prescription for how to think or behave, but more of a simple depiction of what I've found to be true about life.

When you aren't afraid of your emotions and you don't take it all so seriously, Being Human is infinitely easy and unbelievably wonderful.

THE STRUCTURE OF THIS BOOK

Most of the essays in this book were originally published in my free weekly newsletter (which you can receive by visiting www.DrAmyJohnson.com), on my blog, or on other websites and blogs around the net.

In addition to the short essays, there are several *Conversations with Clients* which are—you guessed it—segments of real email exchanges I had with clients. I've included portions of conversations that exemplify the ideas in the essays so that you can see how a real conversation on that topic might (and did) actually go. The conversations highlight how people grapple with applying these principles to their everyday life. You'll be able to relate to many of the client concerns discussed in those conversations, which will help you get these truths on a much deeper level. The *Conversations with Clients* sections are designed to facilitate your own personal insights.

Although I've stripped the conversations of any identifying information, I still asked each client's permission before sharing our chat, just for good measure. They each said yes, obviously. I work with some truly incredible people, as I'm proud to show you in the pages that follow.

FIRST ELEMENTS

While the majority of the essays in this book have nothing to do with children, quite a few of them do. I write about kids more than, say, poodles or apple trees or swimming pools. Why?

Well, I have two of them. As I write this Introduction, my daughter Willow is 3 ½ and my son Miller is 17 months old. Because the essays in this book were written over the span of roughly a year, Willow was somewhere between 2 ½ and 3 ½ and Miller was 3 to 17 months. Not that it matters to you, the flow of the book, or the ideas I'm sharing—it's no doubt my own hang-ups that compel me to explain this fact (Willow can only say "Mommy waaah" in *On the Night You Were Born* but she's telling stories in *Playing the Game...*will that confuse readers?). So, there you have it. My kids will crawl and babble in one essay and sing and cartwheel in the next. This is why.

But this book is not a vehicle to showcase my own adorable kids. I write about Willow and Miller not only because of the countless things they've taught me in their short lives, but because this book is about those things that are natural and innate to all humans on earth. This book is about our default, underlying state, before programming and conditioning take hold. It's about what's there before we grow up and begin to take our thinking too seriously; before we become overly identified with a *self*, and before it's possible that that self is anything less than perfect. It's about Being Human in the purest sense.

I've just happened to live with a couple little people still tapped into to their factory default settings for the past few years. There is simply no better way to see what is natural and innate than to observe children—so in some of these essays, we'll observe mine.

The ancient Chinese philosopher Chuang Tzu explained why children are such wonderful teachers of what is innate when he described the "first elements" that underlie all of human life:

"You want the first elements?

The infant has them.

Free from care, unaware of self,

He acts without reflection,

Stays where he is put,

Does not know why,

Does not figure things out,

Just goes along with them,

Is part of the current.

These are the first elements! "[2]

Unaware of self... Can you imagine not being constantly aware of yourself? You catch glimpses here and there, especially when you are fully absorbed in a task or taking care of another living thing. It's as if "you" have melded with the world around you. The absence of "Am I doing the right thing?" "What do they think of me?" "What should I do next?" feels pretty incredible. Babies and very young children live there.

He acts without reflection... Young children don't think about what they are going to do, they simply act, without reflection, analysis, and judgment. As you'll read throughout this book, simply doing what you feel compelled to do with a minimum of personal thinking is not only enormously easier, it yields infinitely better results.

Stays where he is put... Babies are fully and completely where they are; they aren't doing one thing and thinking about another as adults often are; they are present and satisfied. Grown-ups' constant striving for bigger, better, more, or what could be leaves us feeling empty and unfulfilled. We're left thinking, "There must be

---

2 Thomas Merton. *The Way of Chuang Tzu* (New York: New Directions Publishing Company, 1969). Quoted in Tom Shadyac. *Life's Operating Manual: With the Fear and Truth Dialogues* (Carlsbad, CA: Hay House Publishing, 2013).

more than this"—because inherent in the quest for more, bigger, better is the belief that whatever we have *now* is not enough.

Does not figure things out, just goes along with them, is part of the current...Babies innately know that life flows through them. There is very little they have to do, which is good news because there is so little they *can* do. Something shifts as we grow up and become capable of reasoning, figuring, and manipulating—we assume we can do a better job at life than the life that created us and so we interfere with what is already in motion.

With that, can I introduce you to a boy named Miller?

1.

HOW TO LIVE WITH YOUR MIND AT EASE, REVELING IN THE EXPERIENCE OF BEING ALIVE

"I decided to start anew, to strip away what I had been taught."
—Georgia O'Keefe

There once was a boy named Miller.

He was born a perfect baby—as all babies are—on a perfect January morning just before sunrise. Of course his mother thought he was remarkable in many extraordinary ways, but in reality, he was no more or less perfect than any other baby who had ever been born.

Miller's mind was at ease and he reveled in the experience of being alive.

He acted without reflection. Miller didn't take the actions of people around him personally because he didn't conceive of a "self" that was separate from "them." With things out in the world not about "him" in any way, life was infinitely easy.

Miller experienced life as it unfolded as purely and unfiltered as a perfect baby can.

He appeared to feel content quite often, but he experienced a lot of other emotions too. His parents described him as a mostly happy baby, but he certainly wasn't *always* happy. He cried a fair bit (especially as his parents were hoping to sleep at night) and became angry (at the suggestion of drinking from a plastic bottle rather than directly from his mother) at times. He also experienced what looked like fear (of the vacuum cleaner), frustration (at painful incoming teeth), and disgust (two words: scrambled eggs).

To the adults around him, Miller appeared to cycle through a wide range of emotions quite swiftly and naturally, like a scattered thunderstorm passing overhead.

Miller's mind was at ease and he reveled in the experience of being alive.

As he grew older, Miller began to see boundaries. Faint at first, he nonetheless formed the concept of a "self" as distinct and separate from the rest of the world, first evidenced when his older sister was handed a snack and he ran over yelling "me, me, me, me!" The adults in his life found this rather adorable despite the fact that he was clearly becoming more like "them" (a thought that made his mother proud, but also a little sad).

Miller's emotions began to "stick" as he grew older. Rather than assessing his mood moment to moment, his parents began to say things like "Miller is being silly today," or "Miller is having a tough afternoon." Of course, those statements probably reflected his parents' biases as much as his own evolution, but his emotions definitely appeared to become less transient as he grew more verbal and intelligent.

Nonetheless, underneath it all, Miller's mind was at ease and he reveled in the experience of being alive.

As he grew into adolescence, Miller thought about "himself" more and more, but he always remembered the truth; those boundaries he saw between himself and the rest of life were illusory. Because he knew that, he tended to behave more kindly toward other children and the world around him than some of his young friends. Don't get me wrong: Miller was like other little boys, for the most part. But it rarely occurred to him do things like throw trash on the ground or call kids at school names. Those behaviors simply didn't cross his mind much and, if they did, he usually dismissed them instead of acting on them.

He didn't try very hard to figure things out because—in his experience—most problems in life figured themselves out. Making that his job (the way the adults around him seemed to) looked a little senseless to Miller.

Miller knew that the thoughts that ran through his mind were fleeting and meaningless. He didn't take them very seriously most of the time; he simply noticed them with curiosity or disinterest.

This wasn't *always* true—like all humans, he got caught up in his thinking from time to time. His thought-storms tended to be calmer, shorter, and less destructive than his friends', however, because he understood the fleeting and biased nature of thought. Why get caught up in something that wasn't real and would change in a flash?

When Miller was feeling particularly unpleasant he remembered what his mother had always told him: You're always and only feeling your thinking, and thoughts and feelings are nothing to be afraid of. He understood that thoughts and feelings come and go, and that there was nothing in his experience to fear. That seemed to help him bounce back quite quickly and he rarely felt stuck in a bad feeling for very long.

Miller's mind was at ease and he reveled in the experience of being alive.

As a teenager, Miller had his share of ups and downs. Things didn't always go his way. The girl he loved broke up with him one day and that threw him for a loop. He felt deep sadness, then anger, and then loneliness. He questioned his own worth, like humans are wont to do.

But Miller knew something not all teenage boys know: he knew he would bounce back to the underlying peace and connection that was there in all of life. Because peace and connection were who he was—his true nature—he knew he'd effortlessly return there and he didn't have to actively *do* anything. *He* didn't have to "get over the girl" or "move on" at all; those things would happen naturally on his behalf. Knowing that he wouldn't get stuck in his dark feelings forever made the darkness a wee bit lighter. He still wanted his girlfriend back but, well, such is life. A deeper part of him knew he'd always be okay no matter what.

Miller's mind was at ease and he reveled in the experience of being alive.

As Miller grew into a man, he delighted in life, just like he had as a baby. He embraced change and welcomed challenge, which gave him a somewhat revered status among other adults. They looked at him and thought, "What is it with that guy? Is he not afraid of anything? Does he not care what people think, or that he might fail, or that he could lose everything?"

The truth was that sure, daunting scenarios of letting down his family or ending up in a van by the river occasionally passed through his mind. But Miller knew that those thoughts passed through all human minds from time to time—he didn't believe they were his alone. He saw through their scary tone and the feelings they brought with them. They were more like shadows on the wall that *only look like* a monster than they were any kind of *real* monster. As such, he dismissed them relatively easily.

Miller followed his heart with reckless abandon because he knew he ultimately had nothing to lose. Peace and contentment were his birthright—they were who he was, not things he had to earn. He couldn't earn them any more than he could lose them, so he simply didn't take circumstances so seriously. Peace and contentment weren't at stake, so life looked rather safe to Miller.

He scratched his head as he watched his friends worry themselves sick over landing the "right" job or as he watched them fail to go after their dreams because "What if it doesn't work out?" or "What will people think?" Because Miller knew without question that he could have a wonderful life regardless of the details, he simply wasn't held back in the same way. He did what he wanted to do and bounced back from disappointment easily.

Miller's mind was at ease and he reveled in the experience of being alive.

Miller was kind to himself. He felt compassion much more than judgment toward himself and others. After all, he reasoned, we're all just humans doing what we believe is best. The way he looked at it, no one was truly to *blame* for what he or she did—what good was blame? Blame and judgment require some objective right and wrong and Miller didn't quite see the world that way. He believed that people did what made sense to them given their current thinking—and he certainly couldn't fault someone for falling into the same insecure thinking that all humans fall into now and then.

So, while Miller lived through the same up and down circumstances as the people around him, his experience of those circumstances was quite different. And while he felt the same dark emotions from time to time, his comfort with those emotions ensured that he bounced back from them very quickly.

Miller's mind was at ease and he reveled in the experience of being alive.

Miller spent his life doing the things he loved most. He played a lot. He loved a lot, worked a lot (on things that felt like love), and enjoyed deep connection with the people around him. He often felt as if he were being guided through life. Miller loved using logic and his incredible intellect to solve puzzles and satisfy his intellectual curiosity, but he understood the limits of his thinking mind. He was often quietly tapped into what he called "Big Mind," and it felt miraculous—like home.

Miller's mind was at ease and he reveled in the experience of being alive.

Does Miller's life sound unrealistic or too good to be true? I used to think it did, but now I know it's not too good to be true at all.

This is what Being Human can look like for anyone—even you—when you know that you are fundamentally well. When you aren't afraid of your thoughts and emotions because you see them for what they are—the fleeting, surface-level, stuff of life—your thoughts and emotions have no power over you. When you don't try to "fix" them, those thoughts and emotions relax on their own and you catch amazing glimpses of the "you" that is always there beneath them.

Your experience of life can be this peaceful. In fact, it's your birthright.

2.

WHY OUTSIDE-IN SEEMS SO COMPELLING (AND WHY IT'S REALLY JUST SUPERSTITION)

"Trying to be happy by accumulating possessions is like trying to satisfy hunger by taping sandwiches all over your body."
—*George Carlin*

I had a fascinating experience this morning.

I felt really good. I was totally tapped into a nice, healthy dose of inner peace. I felt a profound sense of connection—people and nature looked radiant in a way they rarely do. My always delicious coffee was off-the-charts delicious today.

THE ILLUSION

Almost immediately, and even though I know better, I found myself trying to attribute my feeling to something in the room.

It was because the whole house was asleep, I figured. Or maybe it was that there were fewer than 5 emails in my inbox, or because I was reading a book I love, or because I caught the sunrise at that perfect orange moment that lasts less than a minute...

Because I have learned about how thinking creates my experience of life, I intellectually know it can't be the conditions. Yet, like most humans, that's the first place I naturally look. Looking to conditions gives us an illusion of control. If we can figure out which outside conditions create peace we can replicate them and *voila!*... life of bliss.

It sounds easy enough—but as you've no doubt experienced, those feelings aren't actually replicable on demand, and they certainly aren't replicable via the manipulation of situations. It's a little like rearranging your furniture and expecting your home to be better able to withstand a hurricane.

THE TRUTH

Our thinking changes, all on its own. Changes in thinking create changes in mood.

When you look around to attribute a cause to your mood you end up drawing incorrect, superstitious conclusions like "quiet mornings make me happy."

Then you go into your life and start trying to rearrange things to produce more of the same mood. You wake up 20 minutes early every day to recreate that one glorious silent morning, but you notice that other silent mornings aren't quite the same.

You start telling yourself that you "need quiet time" in order to feel good, which causes all kinds of problems, especially when quiet time isn't possible. Strangely, you find noisy mornings less pleasant than before.

Now you're a little stuck. You're more convinced than ever that you know the key to inner peace. But when those talkative kids just won't sleep in, you're screwed. It's not much different from how my husband and his Green Bay Packers are screwed when his lucky Packer shirt gets doused in guacamole and needs to be washed during a game.

LIVE THE TRUTH, NOT THE ILLUSION

The same External-Condition-That-Caused-The-Feeling scavenger hunt happens all the time, and it's no wonder, really.

Let's look at another example. Say you want something you don't have—maybe a life partner.

When you don't have a partner, your thinking is inevitably focused on not having what you want. That thinking creates feelings of lack or dissatisfaction.

Then you meet him. He's wonderful and suddenly you feel amazing. Must be him, right? He is the tallest, most obvious new condition around, and your mood changed just as he entered the picture. It's a perfectly logical conclusion to draw. HE is the cause of your new-found happiness!

But something else entered the equation just before your mood changed. Your thinking shifted. Suddenly you weren't focused on not having a partner; you were focused on how lucky you are to have met Mr. Perfect.

And so your feelings changed. But in our superstitious thinking, we look outside before we look inside. The handsome stranger is easier to see than that shift in thinking, although the shift in thinking is the real game changer. It is what changed inside you, not what changed outside you, that changed how you felt and affected your experience of life. Things out in the world can't possibly create feelings within us. It simply doesn't work that way—despite the fact that it always *looks like* it works that way.

Shifts in thinking (and thus shifts in feeling) happen all the time. They are effortless and free. They don't require that you wake up 20 minutes early or spend your weekend on eHarmony. Wake up early and join eHarmony if you feel compelled to do so, by all means. But do so knowing that those actions aren't the direct cause of any happiness you might experience.

A shift in thinking is...and a shift in thinking is available in any moment.

3.

HOW TO TAP INTO YOUR INFINITE WISDOM

"What can we gain by sailing to the moon if we are not able to cross the abyss that separates us from ourselves?"
—*Thomas Merton*

"Slow down and everything you are chasing will come around and catch you."
—*John De Paola*

My almost three year old, Willow, is obsessed with playing doctor.

She lies on the couch, hands down at her sides. She hands me a small flashlight and a toy frying pan (which I'm told to pretend is a stethoscope), and orders, "Check me out, Doctor Mommy!"

She methodically points out every scratch, scrape, bruise, and freckle on her body. She tells me how much snot she feels in her nose and how many times she coughed, sneezed, and hiccupped that day so that I can give her the most comprehensive treatment possible.

After I go through the doctor motions to her satisfaction, she wants to know how her scratches, bruises, and hiccups will really go away. Since we're only playing and mommy is not a *real* doctor, how will her perfect health be restored?

I tell her there is nothing she has to do. Her natural state is perfect health. Her body will tend to return there with no effort on her part.

That's often, but not always, true of the physical body. Bodies always attempt to heal, but they don't always return to how they once were. A body is a machine with a roughly 80-year warranty. It is amazing and largely self-correcting, but it's not foolproof.

Minds, on the other hand, are different. I believe mental health and mental clarity are present in all of us, all of the time.

Sometimes we experience mental health and clarity and sometimes we don't, just like sometimes we experience sun and sometimes we don't. The sun is always there behind the clouds. Mental clarity and wisdom are always there, behind our *thoughts*.

Just like the clouds will always part to reveal the sun, thoughts roll in and thoughts roll out.

Your healthy mind will always return to a state of wellbeing if you don't interfere.

As it turns out, not interfering is easier said than done.

STEPPING IN

Just shy of three, Willow already buys into the notion that humans can "do" life better than the divine intelligence that created us.

She wasn't always this way.

Nine months ago when her brother was born, she was completely unconcerned when he cried. She looked at the adults in her life—tripping over ourselves to quickly calm the crying baby—as if we were crazy. She seemed to be saying, "Babies cry, you know. What's the problem?"

But Willow's brain is rapidly changing. Nine months later, she's in a different stage of development—more intelligent, more verbal, more logical, more action oriented.

Now she wants to know *why* he's crying. What outside, external event caused his emotion? (She already mistakenly believes that emotions are caused by external events—a misunderstanding she learned from every adult around her.)

She wants him to stop crying and she believes there is something we can and should *do* to *make* him stop.

When she looks at me hopeless and frustrated and says, "Can you *pleeease* make Miller stop crying?" I tell her to just wait a minute. Unless he is hungry or in physical pain, he cries only as long as he feels genuine emotion, which is never longer than a minute or two. Then a brand new emotion rushes in to take that one's place.

At only nine months old, Miller isn't verbal; so when he feels emotion, it's clean. It swiftly runs its course through his body, unimpeded by thought.

He doesn't hold grudges. He doesn't have a hard time forgiving. He doesn't remember the past or worry about the future. He just exists in the now, feeling what he feels, before moving on to whatever is next.

Stepping in and "fixing" a thought or emotion is rarely necessary. There is nothing to fix when you allow them to simply roll in and roll out, just like the clouds.

There is simply nothing to do but wait.

BEYOND THOUGHT

Nearly three-year-old Willow has a lot of advantages over nine-month-old Miller.

She can communicate verbally. She can solve more complex problems. She is starting to understand jokes and sarcasm. Her brain can coordinate jumping and running and cartwheeling.

And nine-month-old Miller has a lot of advantages over Willow.

He is more tapped into the wisdom that lies beneath thought. His true state is more accessible to him.

He lives entirely in the present moment, in a perpetual state of readiness to respond to whatever comes his way.

One way isn't better than the other. I'm certainly not knocking the importance or the fun of having higher intelligence.

And using intellect and wisdom gives us a much deeper connection between mind and spirit.

It's just that, ideally, we could use our minds in both ways. We could use logic and words when we need them, and then wipe the slate clean and return to our natural state of innate wisdom when clarity and peace are what we want.

WIPING THE SLATE CLEAN

How do you tap into the clarity and wisdom that lies underneath thought? How can you wipe the slate clean?

Some people meditate. Some people take a walk, practice an art, or take a nap. Any of those can do the trick if you enjoy them, but you don't *have to* do any of them.

In my experience, the best way to return back to that default state where my baby boy lives is to simply understand the nature of thought.

Understand that thought is fluid and that you are not your thoughts. You are something much, much bigger.

As many spiritual teachers say, you are the one noticing your thoughts. You are the nonphysical force that is able to sit back and notice life happening around you. You can observe thought happening inside of you and remain aware of and detached from it all.

When you lean back into your spiritual nature and allow your human psychology (thoughts and emotions) to simply do what they do, you are free. You can watch the endlessly fascinating movie that is your life taking place without getting emotionally hooked into it. *You* are much bigger than that movie.

When you don't cling to thought as if it is true, the slate is wiped clean and your mind goes back to its natural, peaceful state.

You have to be willing to be wrong about everything you know.

It's then that you catch a glimpse of the innate perfection in the system. You tap into the peace and clarity that lies beneath thought, and you find yourself there.

It doesn't matter how old you are or how long you've been away.

It's effortless for Miller, but it's accessible to all of us. Whether you were there just months ago like Willow, or whether it has been decades, peace and clarity are always only a thought away.

4.

THOUGHTMARES

"Thought creates the world and then says, 'I didn't do it.'"
—David Bohm

"How strange when an illusion dies. It's as though you've lost a child."
—Judy Garland

Scary thoughts are not much different than nightmares.

When you wake up after a horrible nightmare and realize it was a dream, the emotion begins to fade pretty quickly. There might be some lingering adrenaline throughout the morning, but rarely much.

"It was just a nightmare. It's not real," is something you might say with great relief.

What if you substitute the word "thought" for "nightmare" in that phrase? What if we treated thought the same way we treat nightmares?

In my understanding, they are exactly the same.

In dreams, stored knowledge and memories are recruited to create a mental experience that looks and feels extremely real.

Daytime thinking happens the same way, except incoming sensory information is recruited as well. Because incoming sensory information helps paint the picture—or maybe just because you're awake—thoughts might *appear* more real than dreams. But I'm not sure they are.

If you are having a nightmare that your house is burning down and you're running around frantically trying to save everyone, and then you wake up and realize it was just a dream, you don't jump out of bed and herd everyone outside. There is no need to act on it because it's not real.

And there is no need to act on all of your thoughts. Just because thoughts like, "I might lose my job" or "The kids might get hurt" float into your mind doesn't mean they require action. They don't demand elaboration or worry and they aren't necessarily warnings or precautions.

They are just daytime thought. And only as real as nightmares.

5.

ON THE NIGHT YOU WERE BORN

"God, disguised as a myriad things and playing a game of tag has kissed you and said, 'You're it. I mean, you're really IT!'"
—Hafiz

Willow got a book from her aunt. It wasn't even an intentional gift; I found it thrown in with a bag of art supplies and hand-me-downs, all nonchalant-like.

It's called *On the Night You Were Born*.

I read it to her the other day. It begins:

On the night you were born,
The moon smiled with such wonder

That the stars peeked in to see you
And the night wind whispered,
"Life will never be the same."

Because there had never been anyone like you...ever in the world.

So enchanted with you were the wind and the rain
That they whispered the sound of your wonderful name...

The whole world came together to celebrate, on the night you were born. I read those words to my daughter with complete and utter knowing that every word was true. After all, I was there on the night she was born and I actually heard the wind whispering her name. The moon did shine brighter. I saw the stars peek in the window to see her.

She believed it, no questions asked. She knows her worth.

Do you know yours?

...never before in story or rhyme (not even once upon a time) has the world
ever known a you, my friend, and it never will, not ever again...

Never another you, not before and not again. This is true of my babies, your babies, me, you. The world never has and never will know another you.

Can you feel the truth in that? It's kind of incredible, isn't it?

So whenever you doubt just how special you are
And you wonder who loves you, how much and how far,
Listen for geese honking high in the sky.
(They're singing a song to remember you by).

Or notice the bears asleep at the zoo.
(It's because they've been dancing all night for you!)...

The moon and the geese and the wind and the polar bears, all celebrating her! Of course they were. My perfect, innocent little baby was clearly worthy of all of that glee—and she believes me when I tell her that.

Do you know they celebrated you, too, with the exact same exhilaration? And the grumpy old man down the street and the ex who cheated on you and you...you, you, you....

Much as I tried to hold it together, I cried as I read to my daughter.

She observed, "Mommy waaah," with her imitated crying noise. "Mommy sad?"

I told her Mommy was very, very happy that I got to be there the night she was born and see the celebration that ensued. And that I get to spend this lifetime with her, the only her there ever was and ever will be.

And I told her I was also a little sad that some people don't remember that the geese honk and the moon shines for them. Sometimes, when people grow up, they forget. Or they can't believe it, no matter how hard they try. No matter how many people tell them, sometimes adults just can't let it in. Some people don't remember how special they are.

At my request, she promised with a pinky swear that she would always remember. She has no idea how difficult it might become as her mind grows up to tell stories and then believe those stories.

Or how difficult it might be when she feels the standards and judgments of the world around her. But she promised to try, anyway.

Can you try, too? It's not too late to try to see it all as a celebration of you.

If the moon stays up until morning one day,
Or a ladybug lands and decides to stay,
Or a little bird sits at your window awhile,
It's because they're all hoping to see you smile...[3]

---

3   Nancy Tillman, *On the Night You Were Born* (New York: Feiwel & Friends, 2010).

6.

BIG MIND, LITTLE MIND

"Life is a series of natural and spontaneous changes. Don't resist them—that only creates sorrow. Let reality be reality. Let things flow naturally forward in whatever way they like."
—*Lao Tzu*

I included an essay in my first book, *Modern Enlightenment*, called "Whose Underwear Are You Wearing?" It was a manifesto of sorts at the time.

In it I shared my seemingly-wacky-but-actually-quite-sound theory that if we all did exactly what we wanted to do with our lives, supply would miraculously equal demand. If we did what was in our nature to do, the world would work like, well, like nature works.

ʌ at the wisdom in nature; the wisdom in ecological sys-
ʌnd planetary systems and the animal kingdom. Look at how
bʌ ʌes are born with their factory default settings set *just right* to
thrive, ready to walk and speak as soon as their brain catches up,
with virtually no human directive needed.

Look at how those innate default settings are always there. You can't
erase the default nature of something—at most you can program over
it a bit, maybe download some peripheral "junk" that slows it down—
but the underlying nature of the system isn't changed. It can't be.

Unfortunately, humans often think we know how to do things better than nature does. We believe our thinking is superior to our
internal guidance. We *say* we believe in something bigger and wiser
than ourselves, but we certainly don't act like it. We fight for Little
Mind to be heard at all costs despite the fact that when Little Mind
is talking, Big Mind can't be heard.

We do it in choosing a career, as I wrote about in my underwear
essay. We ignore the fact that we've loved telling stories since we
were in diapers and choose a career in business because *not many
people make it in fiction writing and the life of a creative is not for me
and I want security and who knows what's happening in the publishing
industry anyway?* We snub Big Mind and worship Little Mind.

And we do it *everywhere* else as well. I talk to people every single day
who *think about* what they want to do that day rather than simply *do*
what they want to do. They logically conclude that they should do
any number of things they're not being called to do.

Because they trust Little Mind over Big Mind, they ignore what
they want and do what they "should." And they suffer like you
wouldn't believe.

They become disappointed in themselves for wanting to rest or play and for not wanting to do the hundreds of "more productive" things they've mentally decided would be best.

I ask: What are you trying to *produce*? Are you an assembly line or a human *being*? Is your life *a production*?

Production is great if you're on an assembly line throwing a car together or engaged in a labor of love in your kitchen. But life is being lived through you. You're here to *be*, not to *make*. You're here to live and experience and love, not produce and engineer and plot.

So here's my new and expanded underwear theory (and I have solid evidence for this, in case you're wondering): When you allow yourself to do what you feel truly compelled to do, life works like nature. When you're guided by Big Mind rather than try to guide by nearsighted Little Mind, everything falls into place.

Tigers and squid and even Homo sapiens babies allow their factory default settings to move them through life with the ordinary flow of nature. You can too.

When you rest when you want to rest and play when you want to play, you will wake up one day and *effortlessly* clean or exercise or return phone calls or pay bills if those things are ultimately in your nature. But when you force yourself to do things you don't want to do and deprive yourself rest and play, you screw it all up. You're playing God, glorifying Little Mind, and doubting Big Mind.

Studies even show that when small children are allowed to eat anything they want, they only eat ice cream and cookies for a couple days before their choices balance out naturally.

Big Mind takes care of balance—balance is not your job. Your job is to do what you feel called to do when you feel called to do it. Trust it. Set the thinking and reasons aside and allow yourself to make easy, natural choices.

Something bigger and wiser will take care of the rest, and your life will be easier and more fulfilling for it.

When you do what you want, life works like nature

Amy Johnson

7.

"MAKING UP" YOUR MIND AND ALLOWING IT TO CHANGE

"We can know only that we know nothing. And that is the highest degree of human wisdom."
—*Leo Tolstoy, in War and Peace*

"If you can change your mind, you can change your life."
—*William James*

There's nothing more attractive than a mind that's willing to change.

Because think about it—a mind that is fluid and moving, not dug in, entrenched or *made up*, is a guarantee that your experience is going to change. It's a promise that you won't stay upset for long, that things are always changing, and that you'll bounce right back to your innate wellbeing in no time.

A mind that's willing to change is freedom from the mythical and much-dreaded place called "stuck."

I once worked with an incredible woman who was going through an extremely difficult divorce. She had been betrayed—big time— by her husband but wanted him back nonetheless. She was as stuck in suffering as anyone I'd ever met.

As we talked, the source of her stuckness became clear. She had made up her mind that her life without him would never be nearly as good as it was with him. Betrayal and reality (he had no intentions of coming back to the marriage) aside, she was unwavering: life with him was far superior to life without him.

With conviction that strong, my hands were a bit tied. She entertained the possibility that she was wrong, but I'm pretty she was only trying to pacify me; only going through the motions.

She considered the fact that her mind truly was "made up," as in *she made up* the rule that life without this man *must* be worse than life with him. She considered it for a second but...not really. She couldn't see it because it was so inconsistent with what she already decided was true.

It's like the fish who says, "Water? What's water?" Her own verdict about the state of her life was so final and all-encompassing that it was no longer a belief we could observe. It was simply *what was* and *what is* can be near impossible to see.

She will let go of her made-up mind someday and she'll allow it to change. When that happens—when she allows just an ounce of surrender—her inherent peace of mind will come rushing up to meet her.

So, if you're feeling stuck in something, remember: you're the one who made up your own mind and you can always allow it to change. There's nothing more attractive than that.

8.

WHAT'S BEST VERSUS WHAT YOU THINK IS BEST

"We must be willing to let go of the life we planned so as to have the life that is waiting for us."
—Joseph Campbell

"When I let go of what I am, I become what I might be."
—Lao Tzu

The two S's: Suffering and Stuck.

When you feel either, there is an excellent chance that you are holding on to something you *think* is best for you...but is really not.

That dream you say is yours (the career you grew up knowing you'd choose, the hobbies and lifestyle you think you're supposed to have)...it's not really *your* dream. At least not right now, right here, in this way.

That lifeline you're clutching (the relationship you're trying to make work, the income and security you say you need) is not actually saving you. It's holding you back.

If the beliefs, dreams, or ideas you're clutching were yours for the taking, they would feel like home. They wouldn't necessarily feel easy or be without obstacle, but they wouldn't feel like forcing something to fit that doesn't.

They would feel authentically you.

Do they? If not, are you ready to let them go?

CONVERSATIONS WITH CLIENTS

D:

"I guess I'm struggling to know when to listen to that inner voice as a good guide—a moral compass, if you will—and when to ignore it because it's meaningless. It sounds like you're saying that the voice is almost always bunk...but how do you ever really know?"

A:

"Inner wisdom (that's how I'll refer to the class of stuff you might want to listen to) comes in many forms, such as common sense (e.g., 'That's just what made sense to me') and instinct (e.g., 'I don't know why I did it, I just did') which tend to be far less verbal or 'chatty' than your run-of-the-mill thinking.

"Inner wisdom is your default nature, always there, *before* thought. It's the knowing that is present before the mental chit-chat begins. In other words, if you're already in deep in mental chatter, you're probably no longer in inner wisdom.

"Inner wisdom is always kind; random thought is not. If it's worth listening to, it will never put you down, shame you into action, or use fear as a tactic. 'You better make sure those people aren't mad at you. You probably offended them,' is not the voice of inner wisdom.

"Inner wisdom might say, 'Call Bill and check in with him.' Or, more likely, you might find yourself dialing Bill's number and initiating a conversation without the verbal directive to do so. Inner wisdom is pure love, so it will never be unkind. It might tell you things you don't want to hear, like 'Get out of that alley now,' or 'Go get a mammogram,' but it's not going to scare you into action with elaborate fantasies of being attacked or being sick.

"Our conditioning has us believe that negative or fearful thinking, or the thinking we have when we're in a low mood, is more accurate than our happier thinking. The opposite is actually true. Thought tinged with fear or strong emotion is totally suspect. Wisdom is relatively calm and emotionless.

"Inner wisdom is patient. It's not in a hurry like random thought. You don't need to do it 'today, or else.' It knows that all things happen in divine timing and it is 100% present-moment focused. The present moment might involve planning for the future, but you're still planning from within this moment.

"The huge, defining, granddaddy difference is *how they feel*. When inner wisdom tells you to get a mammogram or stay out of the alley, it does so with a feeling of peace and certainty. There is no freaking out. There is no back-and-forth mental chit-chat that has your emotions bouncing all over the place. Those are sure signs of ego-based thinking."

9.

BOUNCING BACK

"People who seem to fall apart at the slightest provocation are convinced that their thinking is real. People who are resilient and resourceful in the face of hardship and crisis intuitively know that their thinking is an illusion."
—Jamie Smart in Clarity: Clear Mind, Better Performance, Bigger Results

Humans are *seriously* resilient.

We talk a lot about children being resilient; especially, it seems, after we think we've done something to hurt them.

But actually, all humans have the capacity for incredible resiliency. Given that our true nature is wellbeing—and that the only thing that can ever hide that wellbeing is thought—we're always only a thought away from bouncing right back to our default state.

Resiliency looks easier for kids because they tend to have less thinking in the way.

Without a lot on your mind, you just bounce back. More accurately, you are bounced back. It's not like you have to do it; it's what naturally happens.

With a lot on your mind, bouncing back is interfered with by your own thoughts.

When you're lost in your subjective ideas about why you feel the way you do, how long it will take to recover, and what it means that you haven't already, you're standing in the way of the natural way of things. Attachment to all of that personal thought adds noise to the self-correcting system.

As is the case for all things natural and innate, our natural resiliency is easiest to see in children. Have you ever noticed how children have a really hard time staying mad?

Willow grabs a toy out of Miller's hands and he screams and stomps away. Or he pulls her hair and she takes all of her toys to the other side of the room and sits with her back to him.

About 3.5 seconds later they're playing happily together again.

I remember it as a kid myself. I'd swear I was never going to talk to one of my parents again. I was going to lock myself in my room for as long as it took for them to come begging for forgiveness.

It usually lasted 20 minutes; thirty, tops. It wasn't like *I* changed my mind—my mind changed, as minds always do, and I didn't fight it because I wasn't so wrapped up in personal thinking about what it all meant.

My resilient wellbeing was right there under the surface and I'd be bounced right back into it in no time.

Take a minute to appreciate your natural resiliency. The next time you're upset, notice yourself start to bounce right back to default effortlessly.

But don't blink—when you're not standing in the way, it happens in a flash.

10.

WHY BAD MOODS AREN'T AS BAD AS YOU THINK

"Most of the shadows in life are caused by standing in our own sunshine."
—Ralph Waldo Emerson

How many times have you heard "Follow your heart" or "Let emotion be your guide"?

Too many to count, I'd bet.

It's generally good advice—it's certainly wiser to follow your own feelings than to blindly do what other people think you should do.

But reading into your emotions can also lead you astray. You see, you are always feeling your thinking. You are not necessarily always feeling the truth.

Every emotion, feeling, or mood you experience follows directly from the thinking you are experiencing. That thinking is not always accurate or important. It does not always indicate what's best for you.

In reality, your feelings are nothing more than feedback about your thinking. Feelings are not feedback about your mental health, the state of your life, or whether you have the "right" job, partner, or friends.

I used to think they were. When something in my environment seemingly aroused negative emotion in me, I'd jump into action. Life became a game of adding in the "right stuff" and subtracting out the "wrong stuff" in order to feel as good as possible.

I thought this was very enlightened; after all, I was no longer willing to put up with what didn't feel good and I was consciously choosing more of what did.

For example, I'd notice some negative feelings about my job and immediately start looking for a new one. Clearly, my job wasn't a good fit. I deserved a job where I could be nearly-always happy, I reasoned.

Predictably (in hindsight), the moment I decided the job wasn't a good fit, a million examples of how it wasn't perfect would show up—things I had never noticed before. I took those as "signs"; further evidence that I had better focus on that exit strategy—fast.

Since I decided that my job was the cause of my distress and that I'd feel much better when I found a new one, that naturally led to the conclusion that that I wouldn't feel better *until* I was in that new job. I innocently set things up so that I couldn't possibly be happy until I made the change that was supposed to fix everything.

I also did this in reverse, by the way, adding in more of the good-feeling "stuff" that I thought was the source of the positive emotions I craved.

Although I thought this was an enlightened way to be, hunting and gathering good-feeling "stuff" and playing whack-a-mole with bad-feeling "stuff," it was based on the gigantic illusion that my feelings were based on my surroundings.

In truth, my feelings were simply feedback about my thinking, and my thinking was not dictated by my job or anything else outside of myself.

Thinking isn't dictated by anything. It just arises, with emotion tagging along, and we hold on to it and tell stories about it.

Or we don't.

NOTHING NEEDS TO BE DONE

Rather than jumping into addition or subtraction action, relax. There is nothing to do with or about bad feelings. Because thoughts are transitory, impersonal, and always in motion, feelings are too.

The word emotion means *in motion*, as in always moving.

From the time you woke up this morning to right now, you've probably had a few hundred thousand thoughts and feelings to which you paid virtually no attention. Paid no attention, they promptly floated away—in motion—and were replaced by new thoughts and feelings.

Each time your mind drifts from the morning staff meeting to your lunch plans and back to the meeting again, it's happening. Each time you cycle through, "I'm having a fantastic hair day" to "Did I clean the cat hair off this jacket?" to "I hope it's warm enough to go without a jacket tonight," it's happening.

Thoughts and feelings change all day, every day with absolutely no effort or fanfare.

This would be true of *all* thoughts and feelings if you treated them all the way you treat the ones about meetings, lunch, and hair.

But since you're human, you don't treat them all the same. You hold on to some thoughts and spin them around in your mind. You give them importance and meaning. You imbue them with emotion and attention, which are the equivalent of mental superglue.

Thoughts are like breath—when you stop holding your breath, new breath rushes in. When you stop holding your thoughts, new ones rush in, bringing new feelings in tow.

All you ever have "to do" is nothing. The only position you ever have to take is of non-interference.

WHAT'S POSSIBLE

Nearly everyone I talk to wants bad feelings to go away. Even when they intellectually understand that bad feelings aren't meaningful or harmful, and even when they intellectually get that feelings are always in motion, they feel down and instantly try to feel better.

They think I'm naive or unrealistically spiritual when I tell them that bad feelings don't have to be a big deal. They don't have to feel so "bad."

"You don't understand *my* emotions," they say. "Mine hit harder than others'."

Or, "But everyone knows *shame* is the hardest to handle," or "I've had these since birth so they're more real than most."

Fine. And I still say they don't have to be so bad.

The more you understand that your experience of life is entirely thought created and that "you" aren't what you think you are, your attachment to feelings—good and bad—begins to shift.

You connect and identify with something deeper; something beyond fleeting feelings.

It becomes obvious that bad feelings are only your surface psychology; they can't touch who you truly are. You can rest in your true self, which is always stable and always there.

As it turns out, much of the negative experience of emotions is the cover-up. It's when you resist, hide, or try to change those emotions that you experience them as painful.

When you do that, you're playing with mental superglue again. You're putting so much pressure and focus on those emotions that they are held in place. Remember, when you don't hold on to thought and emotion, new thought and emotion rushes in.

I can honestly say that my experience of bad feelings is drastically different than it once was. This may sound insane, but I don't mind feeling "bad" so much anymore.

In fact, sometimes it's kind of nice to settle into a bad mood. It's a little like the comfort you might find in a rainy day once you accept that the rain is a reality and stop wanting it to change.

I find myself deciding to just lie low and ride out the mood, just like I would the rain. I know it will change. Paradoxically, when I approach bad moods in this way they often end up changing before I have a chance to experience them as "bad."

Emotions are naturally in motion. There is an awareness and distance that prevents me from being taken down by them.

This is completely possible for anyone, even you.

11.

FROM NOTHING, SOMETHING. (ONE OF MY HUGE A-HA MOMENTS).

"The cosmos is within us. We are made of star-stuff. We are a way for the universe to know itself."
—*Carl Sagan*

Who are you, really?

I think it's a pretty safe bet that if you find yourself reading these words right now, you see yourself as something much bigger than a collection of blood and guts and skin and hair. You're obviously not your body.

It's probably just as likely that you don't view yourself as your brain, or even your mind. You can be aware of your mind—so what's that part that is aware? Perhaps that aware part is who you really are?

I'd like to share with you something about thinking that floored me when I first heard it.

It's that *you*—who you really are—doesn't think. The real you...that awareness, soul, universal energy, or whatever it is that you truly are...doesn't think.

Duh. It seems so obvious now. Awareness doesn't think, brains think. Minds think. But you are bigger than brain or mind so all of that mental chit-chat...it's not actually *yours*.

You're not doing it. It's being done through you. You have no actual ownership of it.

Thought arises within all of us; it just shows up. The same energy that causes thought to arise is the same energy that makes flowers bloom and earthworms regenerate and five-minute-old babies root for their mother's breast.

Thinking occurs to you, but *you* aren't thinking. So every time you show up for our coaching session and say "Why do I keep thinking these awful thoughts?" and I remind you that thoughts are neutral (not awful), it's actually even better than that.

Every time you email to say, "I wish I could change the way I think about this," you're just a little off in an extremely important way.

You aren't having any awful, neutral, useful, or useless thoughts at all. They are occurring within you, as they occur within each of us, but you aren't doing it. They aren't *yours*.

You are only witness to them. It's so much less personal than you think.

Thinking happens the way hearts beat and lungs breathe.

Sure, you can purposely focus your awareness and experience on what feels like deliberate thinking about a particular topic. We do that all the time. But those thoughts still originate somewhere— and from what I can tell, it's not from anything you do.

So relax. *You* don't have evil thoughts about feeding your neighbor's barking dog a bag of dog-toxic M&M's, those thoughts occur within you. You're not generating them, you're just attaching to them and identifying with them.

The more you get that you're only the witness—the awareness within which thought appears—the easier it is to not identify with them, and to give yourself a break.

There is nothing wrong with you or your thinking, because it's not *yours* to begin with. It's so much less personal that it looks.

12.

THE LINK BETWEEN FOCUSING ON YOURSELF AND DEPRESSION

"Not on my authority, but on that of truth, it is wise for you to accept the fact that all things are one."
—*Heraclitus 500 BC*

I remember hearing about some research once that linked self-focus—thinking about yourself a lot and making things that happen out in the world be about you in some way—with depression.

The more you think about yourself, the more depressed you are.

There are obviously a lot of missing variables here. This doesn't mean that focusing on yourself causes depression or that depression causes self-focus. It just means that they are related in some way.

The more I understand the nature of our experience of life, the more sense this makes.

As we focus on our individual, unique, separate self, we naturally focus away from the whole and our connectedness.

We naturally look toward personal thought and identify with it. Personal thought feels real and our thoughts about our separate identity feel like who we really are.

If we're all waves in one giant ocean, the more you focus on your own little wave, the less you see of the whole ocean.

When we're very focused on ourselves, we are also less able to focus on specific others. We may be *sympathetic* but we're a little less *empathetic*. We acknowledge others' personal realities less because we're more wrapped up in our own.

In *The Inside-Out Revolution*, Michael Neill says, "When we stop asking, 'What's true about me?' and begin asking, 'What's true about human beings in general?' we discover things about our incredible capacity for resilience, creativity and hope. People are amazing—a fact that's much easier to see when we aren't looking at 'them' in some kind of judgmental comparison with 'us'."

This is not to say that there is anything wrong with, or abnormal about, focusing on ourselves. We live with ourselves and are in our own heads all the time, so of course we naturally feel as if the world revolves around us.

It's just that being aware of the self-focus/depression connection can be helpful, especially when you're not feeling your best.

Look outward. Acknowledge another person's reality for a minute.

Gaze toward the whole ocean and away from the wave you're riding, and notice how your feelings change.

13.

HEALTHY SUSPICION

"I love what I think, and I'm never tempted to believe it."
—Byron Katie

Your experience of the world is created by your thinking. Everything you see "out there" is not preexisting "out there" as you'll experience it, just waiting for your gaze to meet it. You're seeing it "out there" as it occurs within you.

Because all of that thought within you, which shapes your view of reality, is not always inner wisdom—it is part mental habit, part subjective theory, part tainted by what your great Aunt Betty told you about life, and sometimes even part downright lies—it's a wise idea to not take it all at face value.

...hen it comes to being curious—suspicious, even—about your thinking, it makes sense to be especially skeptical of the thinking that causes you pain, doesn't it?

If your always-there-never-changing true nature is peace and well-being, wouldn't it make sense to be extra suspicious of what seems to remove you from that? To question most seriously the stuff that's not aligned?

So imagine my surprise to notice that people are quite reluctant to take their good-feeling thinking as truth. They get suspicious when they feel good. And imagine my surprise to see that they tend to actually trust their painful thinking *more* than their pleasant thinking, as if it's somehow more valid because it hurts.

Why? The old, too-good-to-be-true story is often to blame: "This great stuff can't last. I'm just waiting for the other shoe to drop."

The bad-feels-meaningful-or-familiar story is another likely culprit: "If I could snap out of it, I obviously would" (translation: It's not possible to snap out of a feeling this horrible).

The thinking that makes you feel awful feels more significant, familiar, and perhaps safer—because when you're down, you don't have as far to fall.

Whatever the reason, *it's so very backward*. Thinking that is aligned with your true, innate wellness has to be more trustworthy than thinking that isn't, dontcha think?

CONVERSATIONS WITH CLIENTS

A:

"Remember, J...any time you're feeling anything other than peace or clarity, you are believing something that isn't objectively true. Your true nature is that of peace and clarity and the only things that can separate you from that are illusion, psychology, subjective beliefs, or lies.

"You're only falling into old thought habits, old programming, and (illusory) fear. The point is not to somehow do away with the thought habits and fears because, well, I'm not sure you can. I certainly haven't figured out how—they seem to be part of being human on this magical planet.

"The point is to recognize the illusion for what it is. As awful and as real and true as thought appears, it's not, really. As horrible as any thought or feeling feels, it's always fleeting. Illusory and fleeting are its nature; it can't be any other way. The uncomfortable illusions are on their way out by the time you notice them."

J:

"I just love this!!! This is transformational!"

A:

"I agree. Changes everything, huh?"

J:

"The idea that if I'm not feeling peace, I am believing a lie...! This blows my mind with its simplicity and the way it feels so true in my heart and in my gut. And then if I just recognize that I am believing a lie and wait, the feeling that the lie is creating will pass and I'll be okay. WOW!"

A:

"You got it. Those cruel thoughts about your marriage, the harsh self-criticisms your mind throws out, the fears about you falling apart once he's gone, the urges to eat more than you need...all painful, so all lies.

"They appear true, but they aren't at all true in the big picture, when you get out of your Little Mind and look toward Big Mind. Big Mind is looking at Little Mind thinking, 'You're insane. What a tiny view of reality you're looking at and calling it *truth*.'

"And as you point out, perhaps the most important piece of the equation is that the thoughts and their corresponding feelings will pass. The only effort required on your part is the 'effort' in doing nothing. Just don't perpetuate the lie and you'll be doing plenty. The lies always pass and there is always relief on the other side."

J:

"I don't have to do anything to help myself but notice that I'm not at peace and take a breath and move on. I really believe this, Amy. I know that feelings pass. I'm really excited to spend more of my life in peace, in clarity, and in balance. I'm 42 and I feel like I've wasted so much of my life in a state of stress, agitation, self-loathing, and pain, all self-inflicted!"

A:

"Innocently self-inflicted, but self-inflicted indeed. And isn't that in itself kind of awesome? It was never the outside world doing anything to you. It was never your husband, your eating disorder, or any of the millions of events that take place out in the world every day. It was always only believing the lies and holding them in place, not allowing them to float away and be replaced with new, more peaceful thought."

J:

"Wow, I see it. I've been so in my head believing harmful thoughts instead of noticing the amazing world out there around me. And this idea that peace and balance really are the normal state of being; that anything else is just my own thinking and not the reality of it, is quite amazing. Thank you. I am ready to live in my normal state of peace and balance now. *Beyond* ready."

14.

DROP THE EXTRA (MENTAL) WEIGHT

*"Letting go gives us freedom and freedom is the
only condition for happiness."*
—Thich Nhat Hanh

Most people I know are carrying extra weight—and I'm not talking about gaining a few pounds.

I'm talking about the mental and emotional weight we lug around with us. We carry it everywhere—like a backpack full of bricks—and it weighs us down.

Personally, much of my extra weight comes from the expectations I have for myself to be more—more present, more productive, more enlightened. Although these might be wonderful things to wish for, wanting to be *more* easily translates into not being enough *now*.

In that way, each desire to be more than what I currently am equates to a few more bricks in my backpack. An extra load to haul around on my back, making life a little harder to navigate.

For me it's those pesky expectations, but our habits can weigh us down too: Watching television that doesn't nourish our souls, eating foods that don't nourish our bodies, and holding on to thoughts that don't nourish our minds. The effects add up.

And let's not forget the hand-me-down beliefs. Beliefs like "Good things don't happen to people like me," or "I'm just not lucky in love."

Or the old memories we replay, or the feelings we refuse to feel that bubble under the surface.

They are all heavy, needless weight.

SO WHAT?

Maybe you're wondering, what's the big deal? So what if you're a little weighed down; it could be worse.

Or maybe you're thinking that backpacks and bricks go hand-in-hand with responsibility. It's your burden to bear; best to suck it up and carry on.

You certainly *can* go about your life with your backpack loaded up. The weight is rarely debilitating—and that's exactly when it can be most harmful.

It's when we are carrying a little extra weight but we are still functional that we become complacent, content, or "fine." We become used to the extra weight, we tell ourselves it's part of life, and we stop noticing it.

But make no mistake: examined or not it's there, on your back, making everything you do harder. Casting a shadow on your spirit. Making life less fun and less joyful than it was meant to be.

THE IMPACT OF THE WEIGHT

The weight from those bricks is what distinguishes children from adults.

It's in how we move. Have you noticed how adults often hunch over a bit? They are struggling under the weight of their invisible backpacks.

The way they sometimes slog to work, schlep through the grocery store, skulk to the gym, as if they are literally dragging themselves through life?

How often do you see children schlep? Not very often, I bet.

Children bounce. They stand up a little straighter, walk a little lighter, look a little freer. You can see the difference from a mile away.

It's in our laugh, too.

The weight from those bricks (yes, the ones you think are "part of life") is what transformed your laugh from the deep, loud, belly laugh you had as a child, to the chest-up, shallow, copycat version you often hear from overloaded adults.

The weight from those harmless, "it-could-be-worse" bricks is also what keeps you up at night. It's what keeps pharmaceutical companies in business.

It's what led you to miss the subtle change in the air between September and October, and the way your dog gets so excited when you enter the room.

For me, my bricks are responsible for that rush to fire up the laptop first thing in the morning when there is so much to love in the raw, unscripted morning routine with my family. My bricks lead to me to feel stress where there is none and make choices that feel like self-betrayal.

BECOMING LIGHTER

I can't say for certain—and I sure hope I'm wrong—but there's a good chance you're wearing a backpack with at least a few unnecessary bricks in it.

Are you ready to take it off?

Step one: Open the backpack and take a good look at what's in there.

What *are* those bricks, anyway?

They are different for everyone. What are your bricks?

What specific judgments, limiting beliefs, painful memories, unchecked thoughts, harmful habits, or denied emotions are in your backpack?

Take them out. Go ahead, it's safe. Dump your backpack on the floor like a bag of Halloween candy. Spread the bricks out so that you can see everything.

Sort through them, just like you would with your trick-or-treating loot. Just like you might make separate piles for the chocolate, the gum, the quarters, the stuff you want to trade and the stuff you want to just throw away, do that with your bricks.

Your "Good-People-Do-X" bricks? They go over there where you can dig into them and explore what they're all about when you have the time and energy.

The "Must-Work-My-Way-To-The-Top-Of-The-Company" bricks? They go in a different pile. Maybe they are grouped with some "Hard-Work-Is-Noble" bricks, or some "Respect-Brings-Security" bricks or some "What-My-Parents-Always-Wanted-For-Me" bricks.

Your "I'm-Not-Loveable" bricks—perhaps they go into their own pile, a pile you don't want to touch just yet. That's okay.

Taking stock of what is in your backpack is a big step. Sometimes, just knowing what's in there lightens the load. Start with opening the backpack and taking a good look inside.

Step two: Let go of the bricks you can let go of now. Leave the rest for later.

Since I've opened, dumped out, and sorted through my own backpack, I've been able to let go of several bricks.

I have totally released my "I-Should-Have-The-Perfect-Diet-And-Exercise-Regimen" bricks, and my "It's-Not-Fair-That My-Dad-Is-So-Difficult" bricks. As heavy as they were at one time, they are long gone now. They don't weigh me down at all today.

There are other bricks of which I am fully aware, but I still carry from time to time. Bricks like "Good-Moms-Love-Playing-With-Their-Kids" and "Time-For-My-Hobbies-Takes-Away-From-My-Family."

I know these bricks are still in there. I acknowledge them when I feel them weighing me down, and I have faith that my awareness is enough for now. That someday I'll be able to *fully* leave them behind, even if that day is not today.

I'm sure there are still more bricks weighing me down that I haven't uncovered yet. I don't know any human being with perfect brick awareness.

For those, I simply trust that when they are ready to be released, they will become heavy enough to catch my attention.

As long as I'm doing my part by staying aware, I will become aware of those bricks when I'm meant to.

Step Three: Remember that the bricks aren't real.

Those bricks in your backpack aren't real.

This might feel like a moot point because they *feel* real. We treat them as if they are real, and we behave as if they are real.

But they aren't. You can't literally spread them on the floor. You can't physically weigh or measure them.

They are just perception—just thought. Like all thoughts, they come and go, wax and wane, feel consuming and then float out of your mind just as swiftly as they floated in.

When your thinking changes—which it always does with time—the weight of the backpack changes. When you see things in a new way, or you have an insight, or you gain new awareness, you just might realize that what felt like heavy bricks are actually more like foam bricks.

Or like imaginary bricks. They aren't dangerous in and of themselves, as long as you remember that they aren't *real*.

So when you are feeling particularly weighed down, take off the backpack and dump it out. Do what you can with what you see and set the rest aside. And remember, even the ones that feel very heavy are fleeting.

15.

HOW TO NEVER FEEL
RESENTMENT AGAIN

"The greatest obstacle to connecting with our joy is resentment."
—Pema Chodron

My client Sam just tried to convince me that resentment naturally builds in relationships over time. He said so as if it were a given, and he's not the first person to argue that case.

It's not a given.

George Pransky's *The Relationship Handbook* taught me the one, simple thing that leads to—and away from—resentment.

When you *focus on yourself* and how their behavior *affected you*, you feel resentment.

When your partner is away on a business trip, he doesn't call, and you make his not calling all about you...

> *He's so selfish to not call you and let you know he arrived*

> *He never thinks about anyone but himself (meaning, he doesn't think about you enough)*

> *His failure to call left you worried or angry or distracted*

...you feel resentment toward him.

Making what *they* do all about *you* is not a wise idea. What someone else does is never as personal as our ego would have us believe, and telling ourselves it is does not feel good at all.

What's the alternative? The flip side of resentment is compassion. Compassion comes from *focusing on them* rather than on yourself.

Specifically, compassion comes from looking past their behavior to the insecurity that must have motivated it.

Instead of "I can't believe he wouldn't make the time to call *me*," you wonder, "What must *he* be going through that he couldn't call?"

Maybe he just doesn't feel like talking to you and, if that's the case, what must *he* be feeling that he doesn't want to speak with someone who loves him?

Compassion is about where your focus goes. If your focus goes toward yourself and how you've been wronged, you're going to feel resentment.

If your focus goes toward your partner with consideration for whatever feelings led to his or her behavior, you feel compassion.

Simple, isn't it?

The next time someone does something you're not crazy about, notice where your focus goes. If it's all about you, see if you can make that shift, even if for purely selfish reasons.

Because compassion is much more fun than resentment.

16.

YES, YOU CAN CHANGE
THE PAST.

"Memory is deceptive because it is colored by today's events."
—Albert Einstein

I know for sure that the past can change.

Your experience of life—past, present, future—comes from what you are thinking in any given moment.

In the world of form...where things are solid and objective events go down in the books, I suppose the past is not easily changed.

But in the world of experience, the only thing that exists as reality is what you are thinking about in any given moment.

What you are living is only what you're batting around in your head right this very instant.

Memories are thoughts about the past we bring into our minds today. Memories are *current thoughts* about something that may have already occurred in the world of form. In the world of experience, though, what's real to you in any moment is what you're thinking about.

So, do you see how the past can change? It completely changes depending on how you are currently thinking about it. When your thoughts about your past change, your past changes.

What happened in the world of form doesn't create your experience, your thinking about it creates your experience.

It's what happens when you spend years thinking your mother-in-law hates you, only to one day find out she's secretly envious of you but is too insecure to show it.

It's what happens when you spend your whole life believing your college love cheated on you (and you make that mean you aren't enough), and then 20 years later you find out he didn't. Poof, the past is radically different.

It's what happens when you grow up thinking you are not smart because in 5th grade Mrs. Smith said you'd never amount to anything, only to find out she was actually talking to the kid behind you. Or that she was talking to you but she regretted it ever since. Or that someone told Mrs. Smith she'd never amount to anything and she was only taking that out on you.

It's what happens when you forgive yourself or someone else. Although the world of form doesn't budge, your experience of it transforms completely.

Is there something from your past you'd like to change? Tell another version of that story.

17.

LIFE WITH NO MEMORY

"I have realized that the past and future are real illusions, that they exist in the present, which is what there is and all there is."
—Alan Watts

"Very occasionally, if you pay really close attention, life doesn't suck."
—Joss Whedon

I once heard a story about a man who had no long-term memory and very little short-term memory.

He kept a journal. By the time he wrote in his journal each night, he had pretty much forgotten everything that had happened that day. He was living in a perpetual state of present moment awareness.

As it turns out, his journal entry was the exact same, night after night.

"Life is beautiful. It's wonderful to be alive."

Is that what you thought it would say?

When we aren't dragging old thoughts into our current awareness, there is space. That space is pure peace. In that space is wisdom and oneness and All That Is. The same wisdom and oneness and All That Is that created us all.

Memories are *current thoughts* about something that no longer exists in the physical world.

I certainly wouldn't want amnesia and I'm definitely not wishing it upon you. The ability to store thoughts and bring them into the current moment is an incredible gift.

But maybe the lesson we can learn from individuals who are forced to live in a perpetual state of Now is that the present is pretty damn good. When there's nothing to compare it to, judge it against, or wish to improve...bliss is the default.

Good to know.

18.

THE THING ABOUT
MEAN PEOPLE

"All communication is either a cry for help or an expression of love."
—Tony Robbins

I don't believe there are mean people.

There are wounded people who appear mean. And there are insecure people who appear mean.

And yet, it's not like I *remember* this all the time or apply it to everyone I meet. It's easy to have compassion for some people and harder to have compassion for others. As much as it looks like that has to do with them—*they* are easy to love or *they* aren't—I know it's not actually about them at all.

I can see the perfection in them or *I* can't. My experience of someone else is always about where *my stuff* bubbles up to the surface and mingles with my thinking about them.

If we could step into someone else's shoes, experience his or her life the way he or she experiences it, and see the world through the same filter, compassion would be natural and effortless.

But we can never truly see through other people's filters. We try and we sometimes come close. We drop our preconceptions, detach from our thoughts, and connect with them on the level where we are all naturally connected.

We hear their story and feel their pain and all that jazz. And even then, we're only trying on an approximation of their filter. It's not the real thing.

And that's okay. You don't have to *actually* see through someone else's filter. You don't need to know all the gory details of another person's past and how he or she came to be so wounded.

You just have to remember that he or she *has* a filter, just like you do. And that all people are apprehensive in their own little ways, just like you.

You only have to remember that their insecurity and their pain are what lead them to exude anything other than love and kindness. That's not their true nature; it's just the mask they wear when they are scared.

And remember that the same is true of you. You aren't mean. Even when you're mean, you aren't mean. You're afraid, uncertain, hurting—but you definitely aren't mean.

What looks and feels mean is only a cry for help.

CONVERSATIONS WITH CLIENTS

G:

"How do you approach people you don't like? There aren't many people I don't like—I really can only think of one at the moment—but, unfortunately, she is the supervisor on my shift at the hospital this week so I'm seeing a lot of her (and I'm seeing her when she's stressed which, apparently, does not have a good effect on her temperament).

"Have you read Harry Potter? She reminds me very strikingly of Professor Umbridge. She seems really friendly on the surface, but under it I think she's kind of mean. She always seems really happy when anyone makes a mistake, particularly if they're really ashamed about it. When one of the interns came into scarily close proximity with a highly contagious ailment I was expecting her to be worried, or nice, or angry, or something normal, but she kind of seemed, sadistically, happy. How do you think about mean people?"

A:

"I try to remember that mean people are not innately mean, they are hurting. She has whatever insecurities she has that lead her to act the way she does. Realizing that it's her insecurities rather than some essential meanness (which I don't believe exists in any living creature) helps me feel a smidgen of compassion. A smidgen of compassion often takes the edge off dislike.

"Compassion doesn't mean you're going to feel neutral toward her. She's probably never going to be someone you enjoy being around, but that's okay, right? Just like you don't enjoy all foods or all types of music, maybe we're not meant to enjoy all people?"

G:

"Similar to what you said, I usually picture people I don't like as poorly socialized animals—it seems to help me to see the anxiety or hurt that is making them lash out and it reminds me to protect myself while still letting me see that deep down they are good. It's not working with Dr. M, though. I'm sure you're much better at reading people than I am, but I just don't know that she's being mean because of anxiety or hurt – it kind of seems like she enjoys seeing people hurt. And not just enjoys it because it makes her ego feel better, I think she maybe just enjoys it. It's creepy."

A:

"I tend to think that even the most sadistic 'mean' people—the serial killers, the people who seem to love torturing others—have something about them that drives them to do what they do. Whether she was born an adorable, happy baby and then had some experience along the way, or she was born with a temperament or brain chemistry that made her truly enjoy others' pain, either way it's not her fault, right? I've heard people refer to this as 'psychological innocence'—she'd clearly be guilty by societal standards of mean versus nice, but she's psychologically innocent because she's only doing what is natural to her. It's either how she is or it's how she is—she was either formed that way through insecurities and pain or she was born that way with genes and brain chemistry. Either way, I'd bet she's simply living in a way that is natural given her unique inner workings."

G:

"When you say that maybe it's her genes or brain chemistry, that helps a lot. I can see that if it is, it's not her fault. I suppose that even if it is pain or insecurity that did this to her, that's not exactly her fault either. Psychological innocence is a good way of thinking about it.

"There is another part of this that's bothering me. I don't even really know if I dislike her—it's more like I'm repulsed by her, and being repulsed by someone seems like kind of an intolerant response."

A:

"Repulsion is intolerant? Are you sure?

"Emotions are just emotions. They are fleeting and neutral until we label them good, bad, ugly, or intolerant.

"Although it may not be your favorite emotion, can you be okay with a little repulsion if that's what comes up? Judging yourself for the feeling that naturally arises within you isn't helping matters."

G:

"When I feel repulsed by something I usually assume it means I need to look at it from another angle to see the beauty—even maggots, when you look at them under a microscope, are really beautiful. Any thoughts on how to do that with people?

"I could be wrong, but that kind of seems to be what you do—see a person as perfect and then help them see it too. How do you do that? When you're repulsed by a person (maybe you're far too enlightened for that sort of response), what do you do?"

A:

"If you can look at her from another angle and see her beauty, that's awesome. But you may not get there and it truly does not matter. If you're not resisting your repulsion and criticizing yourself for feeling it, your experience of it will transform.

"What do I do? I do everything I mentioned above...I remind myself that the person I don't like was once someone's innocent baby which usually makes way for a little compassion. That compassion tends to help me be a bit less blame-y and judge-y.

"And if I'm still repulsed or don't want to be around them, that's fine. I do my best to allow myself to feel what I feel and then I avoid them if possible. How's that for enlightenment?!

"I know that's not either of our true nature (their behavior is not their true nature and my repulsion is not my true nature). We're both only human. Then I avoid them and carry on."

19.

THE IMPORTANCE OF
AN EMPTY FUTURE

"Looking to the database of the known for navigating the future is like looking in the rear-view mirror to find your way forward."
—Jamie Smart in Clarity: Clear Mind,
Better Performance, Bigger Results

"Whatever the past has been, you have a spotless future."
—Unknown

What's in your future? Hopefully, not much.

When your future is empty—as in wide open, blue ocean, blank slate—you're sitting pretty to put whatever you want there.

Most of us do not have an empty future. Most of us have a jam-packed future. Do you know what it's full of?

The past.

We drag all sorts of stuff around with us everywhere we go. Like a big 'ole ball and chain.

We drag around stories that we made up (and forgot that we made up).

We drag around rigid beliefs that limit our possibilities and don't benefit us.

We drag around judgments that reflect us much more than they reflect reality.

We drag around pain. And from the pain we invent and drag around methods for protecting ourselves from more pain, except our methods rarely work the way we want them to.

We drag all of this stuff from the past—and much more, actually—everywhere we go. Into the present. Into our relationships, careers, and hobbies. And into the future.

If we're not careful, the past becomes the basis for the future. The past severely limits what is possible for the future because the future is no longer wide open, blue ocean, blank slate. It's "this is just who I am...." And "that happened when I was six...." And "things like that don't work out for me..."

Isn't that kind of backwards? The past is done and over and unless you're constantly reminding yourself of it and dragging it around with you, it has no place in the future. How could it?

So how do you keep your future nice and empty so that you're free to create whatever you want there?

Leave the disempowering parts of the past behind you. This doesn't have to be difficult; just notice the content of your thinking enough to recognize when you're replaying something that is o-v-e-r.

Or when you're telling a story that hurts, or reciting your "this is just who I am...."; "that happened when I was six...."; "things like that don't work out for me..." mantra.

And choose to let that go. It's been weighing you down and dirtying up your future.

In your mind's eye, see the future as wide open. I literally picture a huge open space, completely void and empty, stretched out as far as the (imaginary) eye can see.

Then choose what you want to put there. Remember that you need not bring anything from the past along—everything you need will be available to you when you need it.

You get to paint this picture on a clean canvas.

you get to paint the future on a clean canvas

Amy Johnson

20.

SO WHAT IF YOU DON'T KNOW?

"Sometimes questions are more important than answers."
—Nancy Willard

It always amazes me how much meaning people attach to the innocent little state of uncertainty.

Actually, "I don't know" is an innately neutral statement of fact pertaining to a single moment in time.

There is never anything inherently bad, scary, or "wrong" with "I don't know," and it is only true for as long as it's true. You only don't know until you do know.

When the incredible people for whom I work tell me they have a problem, very often that problem starts with "I don't know."

"I don't know what I want to do next," or "I don't know who to trust anymore," or "I don't know which path to choose."

You don't know right now. So what? Is it possible that you don't know now but you will know soon? That you don't know now but you'll know when you know?

And is it possible that you don't know now and you won't know for a while, but not knowing won't matter? Is it possible that although your rational, linear mind *wants* to know so it can tie this thing up with a nice red bow, knowing right now isn't actually required?

As far as I can tell, distaste for "I don't know" is rooted in two primary incorrect assumptions.

One: There is something you have to do in order to know.

What if you're not responsible for getting yourself to knowing? In my understanding, thought arises within us. Knowing is just thought—you don't have to make yourself know or think any more than you have to make yourself breathe or digest.

"I'm full" doesn't look like a problem because you aren't responsible for becoming less full. Nature digests your lunch with no deliberate effort on your part. You can just kick back and wait.

Could "I don't know" be the same as "I'm full"? "I don't know now, but I'll wait and I'll probably know later," you'd say. How easy is that?

Two: If you don't know now you'll be stuck in "I don't know" forever. And that will somehow matter.

It's not possible to be stuck with no new thought—at least, not for long. Again, new thought arises and it arises often. When you're not holding onto old thought, new thought just walks right through the front door.

Yes, I did say that you have to not hold on and, yes, that's often mistaken as "something to do." (You really want to make work for yourself, don't you?) So here's some help on that—when you go around repeating: "I don't know; I mean, I have absolutely no clue! What should I do? What *can* I do? I don't have the foggiest!" you might be holding on to your "I don't know" thought a wee bit. So stop that, if you need something to do.

"I'm full" isn't a problem because becoming less full is not your job, and it's also not a problem because you know that you won't be full forever. Just stop eating and wait; "I'm full" is wholly self-correcting.

Could "I don't know" be wholly self-correcting too?

WHEN "I DON'T KNOW" IS FUN

Further confirming its inherent neutrality, there are times when "I don't know" is exciting and fun.

When I'm playing "Will-we-see-a-slug-bug-before-we-get-there?" in the car with Willow, "I don't know" is the whole point. "We're almost home and I don't see one yet!" she squeals with delight.

"We're 3 minutes from home. Guess—will we see one or not?"

"Ooh, I don't know!!!" She positively revels in not knowing. It's an adventure, certainly not the problem it is for many of us linear-thinking grown-ups.

Willow knows she's not responsible for slug bug appearances. There's nothing for her to do but keep her eyes glued to the window. There is nothing at stake but bragging rights.

Lest you think this is easy only for three year olds hunting slug bugs, it's also fun for my neighbor who is a sophomore in high school being recruited by universities to play volleyball.

"Where do you think you'll end up?" we ask, only to celebrate her possibilities and keep our imaginations busy. "I don't know!" she says full of eagerness and anticipation. She can't wait to find out—but she's thoroughly enjoying every second of the not knowing. It's like a suspense movie in which she's the star.

She will know someday, relatively soon, with no effort on her part. And while the trajectory of her life might be shaped by where she ends up, the quality of her life is not at stake. Happiness isn't about LSU versus Michigan, volleyball versus mathematics, college versus no college. She instinctively knows that, so "I don't know" is a fun game for her, like slug bug hunting is for Willow.

The exact same is true of your "I don't know," by the way, no matter what it is about.

It's not your job to change it.

It will most likely change on its own.

And what you might think is in jeopardy if it never changes (e.g., your happiness, security, peace of mind) is not actually in jeopardy at all.

21.

A NEW WAY TO MAKE A WISH

"Whatever the present moment contains, accept it as
if you had chosen it."
—Eckhart Tolle

Willow and I have a girls' day routine. We go for a long walk and then I take her to a park she loves because there is a fountain there.

She stands on the ledge of the fountain. I give her a penny and tell her to throw it in and make a wish.

"What's a wish?" she asks. (She's two.)

I say something like, "A wish is something you want. Think of something that is really fun and wish for that."

"Oh, okay!" she says, excited about the concept. (*My* wish is that you could hear how she says "Oh, okay!" when she learns something new. It's adorable.)

Then she immediately looks around at what she has. The doll sitting in her stroller that she got to bring from home, the penny in her hand, the sucker I just bribed her with...and she wishes for that.

Same routine, every time. "I wish *fooor*....my doll!" "I wish *fooor*...a penny!"

"Is there anything you don't already have that you want to wish for?" I try to clarify.

She's thoroughly confused. Why would she want what she doesn't have when it's so much easier to want what she does have? Why not wish for what's already right there?

This reminds me of how Byron Katie says the same thing in more sophisticated words. How do I know what I want until I see what I have?

Katie and Willow know what's up. Freedom is wishing for and wanting what you already have.

I wish to be married to my husband.

I wish for peace of mind and moments of deep spiritual connection.

I wish for lots of stressful-seeming stuff to come at me so that I can learn to focus on what's important. So that I can practice finding that calm place in the face of external chaos.

I wish for girls' days and football season and a baby who is inching closer to sleeping through the night.

Voila...got it. All of it, just like that, instantaneous. That's the way it works when you want what you already have.

What do you wish for?

22.

BEING THE PERFECT GIRL

"The thing that is really hard, and really amazing, is giving up on being perfect and beginning the work of becoming yourself."
—Anna Quindlen

"You can be anything you want." Empowering, right?

In her incredible book *Perfect Girls, Starving Daughters: The Frightening New Normalcy of Hating your Body,* Courtney E. Martin discusses how my generation grew up with feminist mothers "empowering" us with this very statement, day in and day out.

My mom taught me this. Did yours?

But instead of empowering us, that simple little well-meaning statement set off a lifelong quest for perfection.

Instead of empowering us, it froze us. Rather than helping us see possibilities in the present, it led many of us to judge ourselves unfairly and hold ourselves to ridiculous standards.

Because while they were saying "You can be anything," what we heard was, "You have to be everything."

We misunderstood their message—big time.

We took the logic a few steps too far, thinking: If I *can* do or be or have anything, something is wrong if I don't do or be or have *everything.*

I don't know about you, but that's exactly what I made it mean.

We must have it all and do it all. And it should look easy and effortless, while we're at it.

It's no wonder we put so much pressure on ourselves. It's no wonder that as adults running a household or a business or both, trying to take care of ourselves and who knows how many other people, we still feel like we're not doing enough.

It's no wonder we still strive for perfection in so many insidious, innocent-looking ways in our daily lives and silently beat ourselves up for not being better than we are.

Therein lies the potential problem in striving or "trying to be" anything other than exactly what you are: it stacks the deck so that who you are right now doesn't look like enough. And that's a lie. It's not possible for who you are to be "not enough."

I don't need to know anything about you to know that's true. If you're alive, it's true.

So, in case you were under the same confusing spell I was for the past 20- or 30-some years, rest assured.

You *can* be or do or have anything you want, but you don't *have* to be or do or have *anything*. Just because you can, doesn't mean you should.

It's up to you. Know what's most important to you and do that. Everything else lines up behind it.

It's about quality, not quantity.

It's about personal fulfillment, definitely not perfection.

And it's about doing the right things for you, not doing everything for everyone.

23.

ON FIGURING IT OUT

"Leave thinking to the one who gave intelligence. In silence there is eloquence. Stop weaving and watch how the pattern improves."
—Rumi

What percentage of your day do you suppose you're in your head, actively thinking or trying to figure something out?

Maybe you're thinking about what's for dinner, or using concepts and memory to solve a problem at work.

Maybe you're trying to arrive at the best way to discipline your kids, ask your boss if you can leave work early, or approach your wife about cleaning her toothpaste out of the sink.

Or perhaps you're planning for the future, visualizing how you want something to work out, or dreaming about your next vacation.

What's your estimate? 60% of your day? 75%? 90%?

Most people I've asked estimate that at least 85-90% of their day is spent in deep thought, analysis, or figure-it-out mode.

Have you seen what happens when you drop the planning and figuring and just *be?*

What I tend to find is that things work themselves out. Incredibly, most of the time when I stop making things my job, those things I drop become non-issues.

When I stop obsessively calling my doctor to ask advice and schedule my follow up, her office calls me.

When I quit trying to mentally construct my next business move, an opportunity shows up.

And when I stop worrying about dinner, we get take-out and everyone is happy. (Okay, I never actually worry about dinner. But my husband tells me that when *he* stops worrying about it, we get take-out and everyone is happy.)

Not only do things work themselves out, but they do so in a way that tends to yield infinitely better results than my limited intellect ever could.

If this is true, why do we spend so much time and energy trying to figure things out? Why don't we just relax into the moment and allow the energy of life to provide insights and solutions as it always, naturally seems to do?

My hunch is that it's mostly because we don't trust it.

We believe our input is needed. I hear concerns like these all the time:

"If I don't figure it out, everything will fall apart."

"If I didn't plan or make things happen, I'd be lazy. I'd have no preferences and I'd be boring."

"If I didn't scare myself into working so hard I'd probably sleep or watch talk shows all day."

Now let me introduce you to just two of the roughly 602,000,000 people on earth who practically never get caught up in their heads trying to figure things out. They live almost entirely in the present moment, following only their feelings about what they want to do next.

They are my offspring. Along with the other 600 million or so kids under the age of 5, they almost never get caught up in their own thinking.

They don't believe they need to put much mental effort into life. They have an implicit trust in universal energy, and they see firsthand that when they allow themselves to be guided by joy, life is pretty good.

Their lives aren't falling apart, even in the absence of planning and forethought and with a minimum of parental hovering.

When they're hungry, they ask for a snack. When they have a lot of pent up energy, they run, jump, and dance. When they are tired, they rest.

They don't think about it because they don't have to.

They don't tell themselves they "should" get some exercise, and they don't count the hours of sleep they're about to get and then predict how happy they will feel the next day. They just move when they feel like moving and sleep when they feel like sleeping.

They have a lot of strong preferences, they certainly aren't lazy, and you would never in a million years say that they do nothing with their lives. They do a ton of stuff with their lives...*way* more than most adults I know. They create and laugh and play and rest and then do it all over again.

I've never once heard them say that they need to plan for their week, yet they do an extraordinary amount of living each and every week.

I've never overheard them trying to figure out how to have better relationships or enjoy life more or focus on their priorities. Yet they have effortlessly rich and simple relationships with everyone they meet. They enjoy a life that revolves around their priorities without even knowing how to say the word "priority."

They do a lot of that *just being* I mentioned, and it seems to work pretty well for them. And for most of the other children I've seen, too.

You're right—they don't have jobs to go to or bills to pay. No one depends on them for anything or expects them to do or be anything other than what they are.

I'm not suggesting that you strip down your responsibilities to nothing and finger paint all day. I'm only suggesting that you remember what it was like to be a kid, before you lived from your head, and consider bringing a little more of *that* quality to today's bills and responsibilities.

CONVERSATIONS WITH CLIENTS

M:

"As I prepare to step back into the dating world, I'm making a list of what I want in my next intimate relationship. My Desires and My Deal Breakers.

"So I'm curious...What are your must haves? What are your deal breakers?

"What do you know now that you wish you would have known then (AKA — what have you discovered is important for you in a relationship)?

"If you got to choose again, (like I am), what would you do differently?

"The most important pieces of relationship advice you have to offer—I'm in it for the taking, please."

A:

"At the risk of this being not at all what you're looking for, here are my thoughts.

ı desires: it seems to me that you like what you like and you want what you want. So why taint those innate, instinctual desires by thinking about and planning for them ahead of time?

"You're designed to have very natural and automatic preferences. When you sit down and try to *think about* what you want, you introduce unnecessary noise into the system. It's like thinking a lot about what you might want for dinner a month from today. The more you think, the more you start adding in extraneous thoughts that take you off track (e.g., Chinese is good but is it healthy? Eggplant is great but will it be in season? Will I be dining alone or with others? What 'should' I want to eat?).

"Why not just show up a month from today and without exerting effort, eat what you're hungry for?

"Why not just show up with people and allow yourself to be drawn to what you're drawn to? Naturally, without effort or biased thinking about it?

"Second, on deal breakers: how could you possibly know today what might feel like a deal breaker when you meet someone? Mentally setting a bunch of limits ahead of time seems to me, well, limiting. And arbitrary. And again, a lot of mental work for no real gain.

"Maybe you don't need to think ahead about what you won't like when and if you eventually see it. Do you think you might just know in the moment?

"I have a hunch that you'll be narrowing the pool of potential mates pretty quickly off the bat, based only on your true and natural feelings. Why think ahead of time about narrowing it further because of how you think about a feature or quality today? By the time you show up with a person, today's thinking is already outdated.

"It's a little like committing to using a map for your trip next month that is based on today's construction and traffic patterns. Why do that when you could just show up the day of your trip and turn on an up-to-date GPS?

"So like I said, this is maybe not what you're looking for but it's what occurs to me.

"Personally, I wouldn't do anything differently if I had it to do again. No check-list, no rules, just showing up with a minimum of thinking and discovering how the deepest part of me feels about the deepest part of someone else. I think that's the safest bet there is.

"Have fun out there!"

24.

DECISIONS, DECISIONS

"In vital matters...such as the choice of a mate or a profession, the decision should come from the unconscious, from somewhere within ourselves. In the important decisions of personal life, we should be governed, I think, by the deep inner needs of our nature."
—Sigmund Freud

It's pretty amazing what people do because they think it will give them a better life.

They wake up insanely early and go to bed insanely late.

They go to college, and they set goals. They work hard or they refuse to work hard. They decide to be ambitious.

They get married or they stay single; they have kids or they don't. They become friends with people they may or may not genuinely enjoy and they maintain those friendships even when they no longer have anything to talk about.

They do things for the story they'll have afterward ("Remember when we stayed up for 48 hours straight on spring break?" "Did I ever tell you how I climbed Kilimanjaro? I almost died!")

They diet, they exercise...or they refuse to diet and exercise. They adopt pets. They plant flowers. They join book clubs or write books.

They plan for the future, save money, and spend money (*a lot* of money) in search of a better life.

They do all of these things and many more in the name of "because then I'll be happier." Not explicitly, of course, but being happier and having a better life is the underlying motivation in much of what we deliberately *decide* to do.

None of the things I mention above are good or bad—they don't produce a happier life and they don't lead to a less-happy life. They aren't better and they aren't worse. They don't have a direct impact on how you feel at all, actually.

Like everything in life, you can *decide* to do them for a bunch of good reasons, or you can just do them. *Deciding* to do them for some reasons gets a little messy because your reasons are rooted in a lot of personal, slanted thought. Decisions are rooted in subjective theory. That's confusing, so let me explain.

When you decide that you'll go to college because it will lead to a better life, you're assuming that college leads to a better life. You are deciding to spend several years of your life doing something for the outcome you expect it to produce. That outcome is your own subjective theory (which is often built upon what other people have told you).

Going to college *just because* is very different than *deciding* to go to college.

When you simply have the knowing that college is the thing for you, there's no decision involved—going to college is simply what you do next. When people ask "why college?" you're caught off guard. "I don't know," you think..."just because I want to, I guess." Or, "It sounds fun," "It's the next step for me," or "Because it's what I plan to do."

You know what I mean, right? The difference between deciding to do something and just doing it is a distinction with which you're quite familiar, no?

Have you ever tried to explain why you're with your partner? I'm always suspicious of people who can give a million logical reasons for something as primitive and illogical as love. I'm with my husband because I love him and because I want to be with him.

I suppose I could create more reasons, but why? It feels a little like giving reasons why you're hungry.

Likewise, if you're one of those women for whom having children felt more like an evolutionary directive rather than a mental choice, you can't possibly explain why you decided to have kids. You *just did*. You *just knew*. It wasn't a decision, it was just what happened.

That's the beauty in evolution, instincts, drive, and inner wisdom— they take your decisions away. Because, let's face it, if you had to make a thought-based, reasoned decision about having children, would you ever in a million years say yes? Would you *decide* to grow a human being inside of you, painfully expel it from your body, and agree to give it nearly all of your attention, focus, time, and resources for the next 20 years or more? Once you've done it, yes, but before you know that love? I don't think so.

It's the same for me in writing this book, my afraid-of-heights client who just rappelled down a canyon, and my friend who hit "submit" for the overly-ambitious job that feels scary but right. If those things were decisions, we would have all said "No thank you." Luckily, they were not decisions we had to make. They were choices that made themselves via something much larger than a rational brain that can compute risk and reward.

Does this mean that anything you're left *deciding* is not the right thing? Not at all. Humans can complicate anything, even when inner guidance takes your hand and offers to do all the work for you.

If you're bogged down in pro and con lists, it often only means that you're going about it the hard way. You might want a reason for something that doesn't require a reason; you might be trying to apply logic because you believe logical decisions are better ones. Or maybe you're talking yourself into or out of something to which you already know the answer.

In any case, being stuck in decision-mode doesn't mean you are doomed to a poor outcome or that your inner wisdom is taking a nap. It's simply an invitation to step away from the tally sheet, give your logical mind a break, and see if a little clarity doesn't naturally come your way.

Remember how easy it has been in the past, like when you said yes at the altar or walked out of your old job without thinking. See if you can allow it to be that easy this time, either way it goes.

And if you can't, that's okay too. In the end, it's only one decision in a lifetime full of them. Although you rarely make your best decisions *because of* your thinking, it's totally possible to make good decisions *despite* your thinking.

25.

JUST BECAUSE YOU CAN DOESN'T MEAN YOU SHOULD

"Beware the barrenness of a busy life."
—Socrates

I have a toddler, a brand new baby, and a business to run. So here's something I've been forced to re-learn: Just because I can doesn't mean I should.

Just because I can get up to exercise at 6 every morning doesn't mean I should.

Just because I can work until midnight doesn't mean I should.

Just because I can take on three new clients and still make time for the things I want to do doesn't mean I should.

Let this be the new anthem of the good-girl, the perfectionistic, over-achieving, must-do-more junkie: Just because you can doesn't mean you should.

I have to know my own raison d'être, and let my own values, priorities, and emotions guide the way.

I could do a million things that look good and sound good—but do they *feel* good? And even if they feel good, are they *worth it*? There are always trade-offs.

If I lived on a deserted island, free of the opinions of others, would I want those things?

If no one ever told me I should strive to be my best, would I want those things?

Just because I can doesn't mean I should.

Accepting that I can but I don't have to means I let myself off the hook for all the shoulds. It involves a decision— a conscious choice—to be fine now, not *when* or *if*....

Because this lesson is showing up big in my life right now, I'm noticing it left and right with my clients. Care to join us?

Just because she can—in theory—catch every speck of dust in the house doesn't mean she should. She has to ask herself: to whom is this dustless home really important?

Just because he can make $167,000 plus bonuses in a job that's not perfect doesn't mean he should. He has to ask himself: Is it worth it *to me*?

Just because she can starve herself into a size 2 doesn't mean she should. She has to ask herself: is deprivation a sensible trade-off for this ideal?

Just because you can doesn't mean you should. What's really worth it to you?

26.

DOES A HAPPY LIFE MEAN A BETTER LIFE?

"Just because you have the emotional range of a teaspoon doesn't mean we all have."
—J.K. Rowling, Harry Potter and the Order of the Phoenix

"The word 'happiness' would lose its meaning if it were not balanced by sadness."
—Carl Jung

There must be a rumor going around.

It sounds something like this: That we should nearly always be happy. That it's somehow unenlightened to have bad days. That negative emotion should be quite rare and reserved for only those times when something truly horrible happens in the outside world (as if horrible outside events have anything to do with it).

I'm here to put a stop to that crazy rumor.

Humans are designed to experience emotions—the whole beautiful rainbow of them, not just the fun, pink ones.

You will never be rid of bad days and, even if you were, would your life really be better for it? Your life would be smaller for it, that's for sure. Your range of experience would be narrower and you wouldn't be quite as sophisticated, for sure.

You'd miss out on a lot of the wisdom that comes from surviving loss and grief and living through something truly frightening. You'd never know that feeling when your cry turns into a snotty, snorty kind of belly laugh. You wouldn't get to experience make-up sex or the peace that comes with hitting bottom and realizing that the sun is still shining.

If you were always happy, your life would be much smaller, no doubt. But better? I don't see how it could be.

And yet, there is still a caveat. It gets even better. Bad days are markedly different when you get that they are part of life. Suddenly, they simply aren't nearly as bad.

Bad days are part of being human. The second you stop judging your emotions so much, there's nothing to write home about. Emotion comes—good *and* bad—and it goes.

You become an EOE, an equal opportunity emotive.

So let's put this crazy rumor to rest.

Carry on with your good days and your bad days and every day in between. Embrace being human and enjoy a big, rich life full of good and bad and the full color wheel.

It feels so much better that way.

27.

THE PROBLEM WITH PROBLEM SOLVING

"All problems are illusions of the mind."
—Eckhart Tolle

"The greatest weapon against stress is our ability
to choose one thought over another."
—William James

The problem with problem solving is that most of our problems are figments of our imagination.

That doesn't mean the conditions we label "problem" aren't real, it just means that the label... "problem"... is only your personal take on those conditions.

Here's an example: If your friend is taking advantage of you, that's actually happening in the physical world.

But the part of you that labels that a problem, and the part of you that experiences negative emotion when you think about it, is *not* in the physical world. That part is subjective, personal, and internal.

Same thing if your marriage is ending, your dog is sick, you can't get pregnant, it's raining on your picnic...

Real in the physical world of form? Yes. A *problem* in the physical world of form? No.

Of course you're not wrong for experiencing these as problems. Experiences are never wrong, they're only experiences. But knowing that the problem is only in your experience can seriously help.

So, I may totally be wrong about this, but I'm starting to think the best way to solve a problem is to start by realizing where the problem isn't real.

It *feels* real. There is some actual event in the outside world. But is the fact that it's a *problem* real?

Look for yourself and see what you find. You just may discover that there's nothing to solve.

The best way to solve a problem is to start by realizing where the problem isn't real.

Ann Johnson

CONVERSATIONS WITH CLIENTS

D:

"Yesterday was my first Board meeting, and it went great! There was lots of energy and participation—I loved every minute of it. But something shifted afterward. I started worrying about how the meeting went and how certain people responded to things and wound up spending a few hours on the phone calling my VP to see how it went and calling a few folks to make sure that no offense was taken to opinions expressed. Of course, no one was offended and I knew that going in, but I made the calls anyway. How do I trust my instincts that a job well-done is a job well-done and leave good enough alone?"

A:

"Isn't it fascinating that you loved every minute of the meeting when you were immersed *in the meeting*? And that it was only after the fact, when your mind started creating elaborate stories, that it occurred to you that anything could be 'wrong'?

"When your story-telling mind was occupied—fully absorbed in the meeting—there was no problem.

161

"Even afterward there was no problem *but for* your thinking about problems. You invented those problems yourself—innocently, of course. Those 'problems' were nothing more than thinking that felt real.

"Think about it: how many times in your life do you suppose you've had those 'I offended them' or 'I hope that went well' thoughts like the ones you had last night? A few million? It appears to be your own mental habit at work rather than a valid conclusion warranted by the situation. It's only your habitual filter, not an accurate reflection of what's going on around you. That's great news, isn't it?!"

D:

"I guess that is good news and it really resonates with me. I always have those kinds of thoughts. During the meeting I was so engrossed in what we were doing that I don't think I had *any* thoughts. But the second my talkative little mind had an in, there she went with all the problems.

"That makes perfect sense, actually!

"So how do I remember this next time before I make all of those embarrassing phone calls?"

A:

"When you get it, you get it. It's a little like asking how you stop being afraid of the monster rustling under your bed once you discover that it's only your cat. Just sit with this conversation and let it take root. There's nothing more you have to do."

28.

A STORY ABOUT PRESENCE: TRAVELING WITH MY KIDS

"Wherever you are, be there. If you can be fully present now, you'll know what it means to live."
—*Steve Goodier*

"Nothing in life is quite as important as you think it is while you're thinking about it."
—*Daniel Kahneman*

Traveling with children is totally enlightening.

I tend to live largely in my thinking. This is my experience: thinking...

"We have three, maybe four hours between wake up time and time for Miller's first nap. Two to three hours once you factor in breakfast and baths.

What should we do?

We should go to the beach. Will it be warm enough that early?

What do we need to bring? Layers; lots and lots of clothing. Snacks. Water; lots of water. Toys.

Let's pack up the car. I hope it's warm enough. Maybe we should save the beach until after the morning nap? No, not enough time. We'll go now.

Did Willow go potty once already? I should have her try again.

Is Miller's nose still running? I hope he's not getting a cold. If he is, we better keep him in tonight. The flight home will be a nightmare if he gets an ear infection.

It's 8:45. 72 degrees. I hope it starts warming up. We should get going."

So. Much. Thought. And did you notice...it's almost entirely speculation about the future?

From what I can surmise given her mood and what she says, this is a close approximation of three year old Willow's experience: thinking (and saying...mostly saying)...

"We're going to the beach?!? I *love* the beach!!

No mommy, I won't be too cold. I can't wait to play in the sand. I love the beach!!

I don't have to go potty.

What's that in the corner? It looks fun. I'm going to go play with it.

I love this toy! This is so fun!

Ooh, what's that moving over there? Oh, it's my brother. You're such a nice baby, Miller. I love my brother (covering him in kisses, so much so that we have to intervene).

No, I said I don't have to go potty, Mommy!!!

Miller, stop taking my toy! I don't want to play with you anymore. Daddy, can you take Miller away?

What? Oh, we're finally leaving for the beach? Yay, I *love* the beach!!"

She shows me what it looks like to live in perpetual creative response to what is present in each moment. She lives entirely inside of what is right in front of her.

She wants to know why adults are so concerned with what time it is.

She wonders why we're thinking so much about the temperature outside. It's 70 degrees in the house, right now. Who knows what it will be on the beach, and who cares? It's not like we can do anything about it.

She can't answer my insane questions about whether she thinks she'll be hungry in an hour or whether she'll have to go potty when we're stuck in traffic. She can't even wrap her present little mind around such crazy talk.

She is fully immersed in, and usually totally happy with, what we are doing right now. She loves the beach. She also loves the condo we're staying in, the rental car, her stroller...

Unless she's not happy; then she's simply not happy. There is no telling herself she should be happy when she's not. There seems to be very little, if any, upset over being upset.

She doesn't personally identify with each and every thought and emotion that shows up so she moves on, always unconsciously and automatically gravitating toward what feels good.

She often spontaneously says adorable things like, "I love me!" "I love my family!" and "This is so fun!" when she's doing nothing in particular. Those random outbursts are her innate wellbeing—that blissful, shared energy that connects every living thing. The stuff underneath thought. Because she doesn't attach to her personal thought, those outbursts naturally reach the surface.

These little people I live with are an endlessly fascinating species. They make it look so easy.

I didn't teach Willow to be this present. Obviously. In fact, my time, temperature, and potty preoccupations are teaching her just the opposite.

But she is resilient.

You'd almost think we were naturally wired this way. Wouldn't *that* be convenient?

29.

ARE YOU DOING WHAT'S NORMAL OR WHAT'S NATURAL?

"The great Way is easy, yet people prefer the side path. Be aware when things are out of balance. Stay centered within the Way."
—*Lao Tzu*

I have a beautiful client who wants to feel better.

She has a lot of circumstances in her life that no one would wish for.

Because of those circumstances, her well-meaning friends expect her to be in constant misery. Her dear, benevolent friends believe that happiness and peace of mind come from the outside-in.

They believe that circumstances determine our experience of life, so it makes perfect sense that they would look at her circumstances and expect her to be miserable.

She buys into their story sometimes. Deep down she knows that happiness and peace of mind are inside-out, not outside-in, but she sometimes uses their sympathy and their outside-in model of the world as an excuse to add to her pain.

Her friends try to help by giving her a list of normal behaviors for someone in her circumstances.

They say, "Of course you are overeating to cope with the stress, that's normal." Her well-intentioned, outside-in-loving friends even bring her food she doesn't need to help her "cope."

Her friends are absolutely right—it probably is normal to use food for comfort. Normal just means that's what most people do. It's the norm, statistically speaking.

It's normal to believe in the outside-in model of happiness.

It's normal to think ourselves into misery when circumstances are tough. It's normal to use other people's sympathy as an excuse to numb out with food or television or whatever is handy in that moment.

And beyond this beautiful client, it's very normal to take your partner for granted and hate your job, too.

But are those things *natural*? No.

Natural means the way nature intended. Natural is default. Effortless, because it's in line with what is.

I believe wellbeing and peace of mind is our natural state. Existing simply, without all the extra layers of thought and stress and things we think bring comfort, is our natural state.

Is it natural to zone out with food you're not physically hungry for? It may be normal, but it's about the least natural thing I can think of. It takes effort. And although it comforts on the surface, it certainly doesn't feel good.

Is it natural to think yourself into misery because you have tough circumstances in your life? Normal, definitely. But not natural.

Is it natural to hate your job and take your partner for granted? When your mind is calm and clear, is that the state to which you effortlessly return? If not, then it's not natural. And how does it feel—like wellbeing, or like thought-based suffering? The former is natural; the latter, normal.

Are you doing what's normal or what's natural?

Doing what is normal will allow you to fit in. It will ensure that you're just like everyone else. You'll have sympathy, understanding, and company in spades.

But doing what is natural will ultimately bring peace of mind and wellbeing.

Sometimes normal and natural are the same thing. Often, they are not.

Which are you doing?

30.

GOAL SETTING IN AN INSIDE-OUT WORLD (OR, WHEN GOALS AREN'T HELPFUL)

"Dreaming about being an actress is more exciting than being one."
—Marilyn Monroe

Here's what goal setting looks like when you believe in an outside-in world: You believe something "out there" in the world will make you happy, so you set a goal to achieve it.

Sounds pretty typical, right?

The thing is, when you're chasing down a goal because you think it's going to make you happy, you're on the hook.

You've set it up so that you can't be happy *until* you get the thing. Or you've set it up so that you will be happi*er when* you get the thing... but not before.

And since happiness does not actually come from stuff out there, that's not an accurate conclusion.

Being on the hook creates all kinds of other problems too.

You end up with tunnel vision, blindly acting in service of your goal. Pushing, working, pursuing...it doesn't feel good and you're not happy. Quite ironically, this thing you are doing *in order to be happy* is making you miserable along the way. (You're often okay with that fact because you're so convinced that *you'll be happy when* you reach the destination that a little torture along the path seems like *"the price you pay."*)

Or...you use the process of working toward this goal to beat yourself silly. You didn't stick to the workout plan or the budget. You didn't meditate every day or things aren't moving along exactly the way you believe they *should*. Now, not only are you at risk of not realizing the happiness that is yours if you meet your goal, you're once again miserable in the process.

Or...you achieve the goal. You did it! But wait a minute...where's the feeling? Where is the lasting happiness that the new job, perfect mate, or "right"-sized jeans was supposed to deliver? It was there for a minute or two. Then you adjusted to your "new normal" and you feel just like you did before the goal.

"I must have chosen the wrong goal," you reason. You didn't actually want to be CEO; you only wanted the money and power. Or you didn't want *that* guy; now that you know better, it turns out you want a different one with a different set of qualities.

So you cook up a bigger, better, more fitting goal and set out to make that one happen. *Now* you're on the right track, you figure. *This* goal will bring the happiness that the other one didn't.

That's goal setting in an outside-in world.

INSIDE-OUT GOALS

Here's what goal setting looks like when you believe in an inside-out world. Because happiness (security, confidence...) are created from within—specifically, from your thoughts—and not from anything out in the world, you don't set goals to achieve things because they will *make* you happy.

Instead, you simply do what feels good.

You're off the hook because your happiness is not at stake. You do what you *want* to do because you want to do it, not because you need it to feel good.

This is radically different than the outside-in way.

Inside-out, the journey is at least as important as the destination because now is all there really is anyway. Thought is the only thing dragging you into the past or the future—when thought takes a back seat, there is nowhere to go. You are here, now, much more often.

You stay flexible. A goal is just a thought about something you want, and thoughts change rapidly and often.

You might change your mind and change your goal at any time. Great.

You might choose to stop working toward your goal at some point. Great.

You might stay the course and achieve your goal. Great.

You *will not* torture yourself in the name of achieving your goal. Why would you?

If you do achieve your goal, you'll probably be pleased with yourself. Then you'll go right back to feeling the way you used to feel. It's the same as if you believe in an outside-in world, except you get to skip the disappointment that comes from expecting the goal to dramatically improve your entire life.

MY RECOMMENDATION

Here's what I recommend: Feel for what would feel good if no one else would ever know, and do that. In other words, focus on what's important to you, not what you're doing for approval or status or security or happiness or anyone else.

Do that, but only if you truly want to. If you don't want to, don't do it.

Make sure you're only pursuing goals for the fun of it. They aren't going to ensure any specific feeling, so don't put that pressure on them.

Change your mind as often as you want. Make a game out of it. Don't take it too seriously and, for the love of God, please don't beat yourself up for not meeting some arbitrary standard that you made up to begin with.

Do what you choose to do because and only if *you* truly *want* to do it. And watch how much easier it all becomes.

CONVERSATIONS WITH CLIENTS

C:

"I've always heard about the importance of having a clear vision and knowing where you're headed. 'If you don't have a destination, you'll never get anywhere,' and that sort of stuff."

A:

"Is that true, in your experience? Do you never get anywhere in your life without a clear destination in mind?

"It may be true for you. I can think of a lot of ways it's not true for me, though. I leave my house on foot nearly every afternoon with my kids in the double stroller and no direction or destination in mind. I have no specific intention or goal and I don't consciously consider which turns to make. I just walk because it feels like the thing to do, and we always end up somewhere. We've never once stayed at the end of the driveway because we didn't have a plan.

"The same was true with my books. I never set out to write two books, I just wrote when I felt like writing and organized my writings into something bigger when that felt like the thing to do—and before I knew it, I had a couple books.

"Not everything in my life feels that easy, but those are two examples of getting somewhere without a map or vision for the end.

"If you're going to be happy no matter where you end up, is a clear vision really all that important? And what if you changed your mind along the way...would that be okay?"

C:

"I see what you're saying. No, I guess lack of a destination doesn't mean you go nowhere, but it does seem like you might miss out on something that you could get to if you put more thought or effort into things."

A:

"There is a time and a place for thought and planning, no doubt. And they can be fun, right? Personally, planning trips is one of my greatest joys in life. Forethought and planning can be a ton of fun.

"I'm just saying that to the extent that they aren't fun or they require a lot of work, maybe they aren't always as necessary as they appear. And anyway, if you are naturally guided somewhere you don't like, you can always just turn around, right? Go back and draw a map at that point, or at any point. Having a vision and using a map is totally your choice; I'm just suggesting that you'll certainly cover ground without one."

C:

"Kind of related to this, do you set any standards for yourself? Isn't it important to have ideals that you try to live up to?"

A:

"I don't explicitly set standards or ideals for myself, no.

"I find that when I'm not caught up in my own thinking so much—when I'm relatively thought-free—I always naturally act in a way that's best for me and the world around me. Deliberate rules to live by aren't necessary—seems a little like reminding yourself to eat when you're hungry. If you're not standing in the way of what's natural, you just eat when you're hungry and you just live by your personal standards.

"So if anything, I strive to not get caught up in my routine mental chatter rather than add more mental chatter about standards and ideals I should be living up to.

"What about you? Do you find that you do okay naturally at times, too?"

C:

"I do find that, yes. My friend Cathy has been working on writing a moral code for herself. Her logic is that so many of our morals are just things that we absorb in kindergarten and often more accurately reflect how our parents and teachers think we should live than how we think we should live. She's re-writing the code for herself."

A:

"I totally agree with Cathy about those hand-me-down beliefs, and that's the beauty in learning to not believe everything you think—so much of it really is hand-me-down. When you don't take everything anyone ever told you as truth, you have a sort of naturally occurring strainer where *what's true to you* floats to the top and what's true to everyone else falls out the bottom.

"I'm just not sure that actively rewriting a moral code is necessary. It sounds like an awful lot of work to program yourself with a bunch of new stuff on top of the old stuff. Rather than reprogramming 'good ideals' over 'hand-me-down ideals,' why not buck all rules and be guided in the moment?"

31.

DRAMATICALLY UPGRADE YOUR RELATIONSHIPS BY BECOMING A TEAM

"We may have all come in different ships, but we're in the same boat now."
—Martin Luther King, Jr.

I once had a totally commonplace, uneventful thought that transformed the way I viewed relationships.

I'm not sure that it was *mine*; it certainly wasn't anything groundbreaking or unique. I may have read it somewhere; I can't remember now.

It was the notion that when two people in a relationship think of themselves as on the same team, things get much easier. Positive feelings grow freely. Score-keeping and resentment are nonexistent.

Insights are very personal—a simple phrase that turns my world upside down might do absolutely nothing for you, and vice versa. Perhaps this notion was so life-changing for me because I grew up surrounded by people who seemed self-focused, always looking for where they had been wronged.

They weren't selfish or egotistical people. They were insecure people.

My father had insecurities that led him to make everything about himself—if you didn't say the right thing at the right time, trouble was sure to follow. I spent years walking on eggshells, trying to anticipate my next misstep. It was exhausting.

And I remember women who constantly, endlessly talked about what was wrong with the "deadbeat men" who never seemed to treat them the way they deserved to be treated.

As a kid, it seemed as if adults everywhere put everyone else on the hook for their own happiness. In my childhood innocence and natural wisdom I wondered: why didn't they take care of their own happiness?

Being on the hook for someone else's happiness not only felt like enormous pressure, it was an impossible task. No matter how much my dad approved of something I did one day, he might disapprove of the very same thing the next day. No matter how nice a man was to a woman, he'd inevitably forget to compliment her dress and she'd have him back in the doghouse.

All of this look-what-you're-doing-to-me, you-should-be-treating-me-better business is *not* born out of independent, empowered women (or men) simply refusing to put up with less than what they deserve. That's often how they like to view themselves, but that's not it at all.

Scavenger hunting for all the ways you aren't being treated fairly is not an act of self-love. It's an act of insecurity.

It's born out of fear and looking to someone else to be your savior. It's born out of the belief that your happiness comes from what others do, which manifests as manipulation, guilt trips, and passive aggressive behavior aimed at changing them so that you can feel better.

"US" NOT "ME"

When you're focused on yourself, keeping score, and making sure you're being treated properly, you're not actually *in relationship with* another person—you're in relationship with *your thoughts about* the other person.

You're focusing on yourself, what you can get, and where your partner is falling short.

Thinking of the two of you as a team shifts your focus. Suddenly it's not "me versus you," it's "us."

It's no longer "I did the laundry every day this week; what did you do?" It's "We're a team. I do the laundry more than you at times, and you do a million other things for me at times."

It's not "If you cared about me you'd call twice a day." It's "I'd love to talk to you more."

The you-and-me-together way of looking at things is exactly what was missing for all of those disgruntled women complaining about their deadbeat men. The extreme look-out-for-myself-first approach is what made my relationship with my dad defensive and inauthentic.

TEAMMATES

A couple weeks ago, I was talking with a friend about her marriage when she confessed that she was once a scorekeeper. She used to keep a mental tally of what she had done and what her husband hadn't, and she gave a whole lot of meaning to that score.

When I asked how she came to leave the scorekeeping behind, she told me that her husband said something one day that completely turned it around for her. In the midst of one of her score reports, her husband said the reason he never thought that way was because he saw them as a team. She gives more in some ways and he gives more in other ways, but why keep track when they are always *working together*, in the end?

She instantly knew that was true. He did give more than her in many ways, but her rigid, defensive outlook hadn't allowed her to even notice what he did for her.

Although insights are personal, she had the same game-changing one I did. She never looked at her relationship in quite the same way again. When she found herself feeling wronged, she remembered that she and her husband were teammates, not adversaries.

Being on the same team takes the frailty out of a relationship. My relationship with my father always felt fragile and temporary, like I was one wrong look away from being disowned. In fact, I was.

Don't you see this in romantic relationships—especially new ones—all the time? One or both people are afraid to fully be themselves in fear of what the other might make of their honesty. I can clearly remember the wave of relief that washed over my now-husband's face when we had a disagreement about 6 months into our courtship. He sat me down to assess the damage and I assured him that we were past the point of breaking up over a petty dissimilarity.

He says he knew in that moment that we were an "us." It wasn't "me" evaluating and judging "him," or "him" deciding whether "I" was right or wrong. We were a team, and teams are infinitely more resilient than individual identities trying to coexist.

I wonder what this shift in perspective might do for you. Even if you aren't a scorekeeper always looking for where you were wronged, taking on the team viewpoint can bring a new sense of closeness to your relationships.

Can you imagine what might happen if we extended this beyond personal relationships...if we saw entire families, communities, or all of humanity as part of the same team?

Imagine how we'd treat each other.

Here's to spreading the insight to our teammates everywhere.

32.

HOW TO TRULY HELP SOMEONE

"Love is what we are born with. Fear is what we have learned here...
An ancient memory of this love haunts all of us all the time,
and beckons us to return."
—Marianne Williamson in A Return to Love

Your rational mind knows this, but this is for the irrational part:
You can't take on other people's pain.

You can't grieve for them. There is no amount of tears you can shed
that will lessen theirs.

When my kids are sick, there is no amount of sick I can make myself (with worry, no doubt) that will make them better.

There is no amount of fear you can feel that will make someone's plight less scary.

I recently coached an incredible woman who was putting herself through emotional hell because, somewhere deep down, she believed that if she suffered enough it might circumvent some of her son's suffering.

It doesn't work that way, and just the opposite is true. The way we heal other people is by staying calm, and connected to our peaceful core, and by not crossing that line into the mess they are feeling.

That messy stuff is not real, anyway. Only love is real, and anything that's not love is ego junk, mental byproduct, human fear. It's all just *psychology*, not *reality*.

Staying peaceful and connected in the face of their terror is not heartless. It's actually the most loving thing you can do for them.

There is nothing noble about diving into their pain. That only magnifies and spreads the pain and freaks them out even more.

Please know, I'm not talking about denial. Acknowledge others' pain—it's very real for them. Give them the space to feel it fully. But by all means, do not jump into their fearful and frantic story and take on any part of it yourself—doing so only gives life to an illusion.

Their fear-based thoughts are only the survival mechanism in their brains running out of whack; giving them more validity or attention isn't helpful.

When I teach people to become life coaches, I explain that their job is to see their clients as the highest version of who they are. That's love, not fear.

So do that. If you want to truly help people, see them as the highest version of who they are. View them without their temporary thought-distortions.

Be the leader by allowing them to stay in full possession of whatever they feel and not being tempted to feel it for them.

There is nothing helpful about spreading fear. Stand in peace, instead.

33.

DO YOU NEED TO
HEAL YOUR PAST?

*"Memories are like holograms: you recreate in your head the whole
image of something which isn't there."*
—Richard Bandler

Do you think there is something from your past that needs to be
healed?

I used to believe that the past required healing. But when you think
about it, how could that be?

The past is over. It's nonexistent today. How could something that
doesn't exist *need* anything?

The past only comes up today in your thinking about it. It's there, I'm not denying that. I'm sure you have current thinking about the past, just like I do.

But if the past doesn't exist outside of your thinking, what's to heal? That's kind of like saying the Tooth Fairy needs to be healed. It's like waking up from a nightmare that your house is on fire and still moving the family outside.

The past is an illusion, just like nightmares and the Tooth Fairy. Illusions don't need to be healed; they only need to be seen as illusions.

No matter what happened in your past, I'd bet you experience moments when it bothers you and moments when it doesn't.

No matter how horrible the past was, it hasn't haunted every single second of your life since, has it? Haven't you still had fleeting moments of happiness? Haven't you been distracted enough that the past was a non-issue?

How do you explain those moments? I'll tell you how I explain them: those were moments when you weren't entertaining thoughts about the past, so the past was not a reality for you.

Your thinking is the sole vehicle for keeping the past alive today. It's your only time machine. So at best, your *thinking about the past* might be healed.

How do you heal your thinking about the past given that you can't control your thinking?

You can't consistently force yourself to think particular thoughts any more than you can stop some thoughts from showing up—but you can understand that thought is fleeting. You can understand that the past is only an issue when you're mentally recreating it, and you can allow those recreations to float away when they do show up.

They float away easily when you don't anchor them in place with your focus and judgment of them.

They will appear from time to time. That's true for every human on the planet. Rather than stressing over their presence, see them as the illusion they are.

When you wake up, the nightmare is over. The same is true of the past.

34.

SHOWING UP DUMB

"I am the wisest man alive, for I know one thing, and that is that I know nothing."
—Socrates

It's endlessly fascinating to me to notice the filter of thought that floats across my screen of awareness.

So much of that thick thought filter is:

a) Basically the same as yesterday

b) Based on something that happened in the past

c) Stemming from beliefs I formed long ago that most likely aren't relevant today.

In other words, old thought runs the show much of the time. That's a bit of a bummer because one of the coolest things in the world is the ability to arrive at today without yesterday in tow.

Imagine waking up and seeing each day totally fresh. Nothing—or very little, anyway—carried over from days gone by.

You show up with a clear mind, open and fully receptive to what shows up. You don't react to what shows up with a bunch of pre-formed judgments and opinions. Instead, you truly and naturally *react* (not pre-act) in the moment.

You allow yourself to be guided through life rather than mentally deciding how life should look and then trying to make things match that ideal. (The latter is exhausting, by the way.)

When you show up without much on your mind, you're seeing the people around without your thick filter of expectations, assumptions, and subjective opinions. You're actually seeing *them*, maybe for the first time.

You can do this in any moment, whenever you'd like. Take a fresh look at your relationship, your work, your kids, yourself. Just look without yesterday's filter and discover what's there. Discover; not confirm.

One of my mentors calls it "showing up dumb," which is a pretty perfect way to put it.

You almost never listen to other people dumb. You listen smart—which means you aren't listening at all.

While they're talking, you're thinking. Evaluating what they're saying, comparing it to everything else stored in your brain, and thinking about what you'll say next. All of that mental action prevents you from listening. That action fundamentally halts your ability to actually hear what they're saying.

When you show up dumb, without all that "What she's saying is like X, unlike Y, good for me, bad for me..."—you get to really hear the person in front of you.

Showing up dumb is a much wiser way to be.

CONVERSATIONS WITH CLIENTS

T:

"... I really want to figure out whether I should have a conversation with him about our relationship or just let it go. Relationships shouldn't be this hard—but what I think you're saying is that I'm making it hard because I'm living in my mind instead of just going with the flow? I hope I'm understanding that this is what you're getting at. I would be better off living in the moment without expectations and over-thinking?"

A:

"Well, yes...put that way, living in the moment feels like a better plan than being full of expectation and over-thinking. But here's what I want you to see: 'living in the moment' and 'going with the flow' don't mean that you don't have the conversation with him. They also don't mean that you *do* have the conversation with him. Living in the moment and going with the flow are not tied to any specific action. Your decision about the conversation *takes care of itself* when you are in your wisdom, rather than caught up in your beliefs and expectations and thinking.

"In other words, whether or not you have this conversation is no longer something you have to 'figure out.' When you step back from the expectations and recurring mental chit-chat, you eventually get some clarity one way or the other. You either have the conversation or you don't. Does that make sense?"

T:

"Sort of, although I really thought going with the flow meant I'd skip the conversation, so maybe not. Can you expand on that a bit just to make sure I'm following you?"

A:

"Sure. Part of living in the moment is 'showing up dumb' as if today is your first day on earth, a brand new experience, without all the stuff from the past that we all drag around with us all of the time. It's coming to this relationship *not already knowing* (because you don't, really) what he thinks, what's going to happen, or what it all means. You show up fresh, open, blank...dumb.

"When you show up without a ball and chain of thought behind you, decisions tend to make themselves. That open space is clarity. You know what to do and you just do it, unless you don't, in which case you simply wait until you do.

"You don't have to think about your decisions so much because you allow yourself to be guided. Like when my baby is crying at 4am and I'm exhausted and sleep deprived and I find myself walking down the hallway toward his room. I didn't make a conscious decision to do that. I didn't have to think about it or reason it out; it's just what happens. Instinct takes over and it's as if I'm being lived by something bigger. What needs to happen simply happens in the absence of my own personal thinking.

"In your case, the only thing in the way of clarity is your personal thinking. When 'What will he say?' 'He won't be receptive,' and 'This conversation is going to be hard' stop you in your tracks, your personal, biased thinking overrides your inner wisdom.

"So, going with the flow is about showing up dumb and being guided into what feels natural. There is no specific course of action. Going with the flow might result in having the conversation or it might result in not having the conversation. It's about showing up without all the thought-baggage and discovering what comes next."

35.

HOW TO AVOID THE UPS AND DOWNS OF LIFE

"The problem is not that there are problems. The problem is expecting otherwise and thinking that having problems is a problem."
—*Theodore Rubin*

Stuff happens in life. You've probably noticed.

Stuff happens to you without your approval and beyond your control. That's the way of it.

Yet, most of the people I talk with want the ups and downs to stop. They are searching for a way to keep life in the "up" territory to avoid the "downs."

It happens all the time. I talk to a client who feels amazing, is tapped into his inner wisdom, riding the wave of life. ...

...until the following week when he's feeling much lower. His thinking shifted and he's fighting it, wanting last week's highs back. "I felt so great last week!" he argues with an incredulous shake of the head. "What is going on?"

Life is what's going on. Thinking changes and moods change. It's really nothing more than that.

It always reminds me of the *Sports Illustrated* curse. When a team or athlete is chosen to grace the cover of *Sports Illustrated*, they inevitably take a turn for the worse.

The team's performance suffers the following season, the athlete gets injured, or there is a scandal in their organization.

There are a lot of lay theories and ton of potential reasons this might happen. Maybe they put too much pressure on themselves after they make the cover and they self-sabotage. Maybe the competition suddenly has it out for them, or maybe there really is a curse.

But the explanation that seems most logical to me is that life is full of ups and downs. When someone makes the cover of SI, they are obviously in an "up." The next place to go is a little down, at least in the way our human minds define "up" and "down."

It's the way life works.

MANAGING THE UPS AND DOWNS

As far as I can tell, there are two ways to manage the ups and downs.

One is to stay in your house, or your little town, with your little inner circle, doing the same things you do every day. Keep your world very small.

This helps you avoid the ups and downs because you will be living somewhere in the middle. When you have few "ups," the waves won't look so dramatic. There's not much to manage when you're on the equivalent of a lazy river—although you might miss out on some pretty fabulous experiences without those "ups."

The other way to manage the ups and down is to realize they aren't real.

"Up" and "down" are only labels you attach to otherwise harmless and subjective feelings or events.

The fear of up and down occurs when you think you're going to be stuck in the feeling, as if it's stable and may not change.

One feature of life is that it is made up of ups and downs—another is that it is always changing. Those "ups" are on their way out by the time you label them "ups." So are the "downs."

The less you cling for dear life to your concept of how things "should" be, and accept and relax into what is, the more naturally the ups and downs do their thing.

The real "you"—the untouchable, only-love part of you—isn't upping and downing. She's safe and sound watching her personal, thought-based identity go on a virtual reality roller coaster ride.

36.

WHAT YOU'RE DOING
DOESN'T MATTER

"God has focused the senses to the outside, therefore man looks outside, not inside. Now and then an adventurous soul, in search of immortality, has looked back and found himself."
—Katha Upanishad

The outside-in illusion is a persuasive one, I tell you.

One day, while working on the very book you're reading, I sat on the floor of my office—Cat Stevens blaring—with 44 pages spread in front of me, each one representing a different chapter, quote, or story I planned to include. I spent an hour of pure bliss organizing, arranging, and numbering them, having brand new ideas about additional pieces I wanted to include, and making placeholders for those to-be-written pieces.

I was extraordinarily content, in the state people call "flow" or "in the zone." I walked away with the skeleton of what I knew was going to be a much better book than my last one.

It would be easy to conclude that my bliss came from the fact that I finished my floor party with an almost-there book I was already proud of. But that wasn't it.

It would be natural to think: Man, I need to do *this* more often.

Or: Creating something meaningful is important to my happiness.

Or: Writing books is my purpose/soul's work/what I'm meant to be doing.

But I know better. Writing, collating, organizing, creating, teaching, Cat Stevens, and my office floor have nothing to do with it. They looked so beautiful because of the feeling I had within me; that feeling I was so tempted to attribute to those activities.

The actual source of my contentment was a clear mind. (That also happens to be what paved the way for those new ideas I had.)

A clear mind *does* feel like bliss. A clear mind is possible anywhere, doing anything. You've experienced glimpses of it mowing the lawn, cooking dinner, and driving to work.

I was trained to talk to clients about when they are happiest and then help them add more of those activities or circumstances to their lives; this approach is based very firmly in the illusion that happiness comes from what you're doing.

It's not that you won't feel better creating your art or watching movies or whatever you like to do. You probably will, if your mind clears. Then—if you're like most humans—you'll promptly look outside of yourself to see what cleared your mind so wonderfully.

You're giving all the credit to a bunch of activities and stuff, but universal energy cleared your mind, the project or movie didn't. The papers or highlighters or Cat Stevens didn't do it for me.

(I'm convinced that this is the basis for most addiction and compulsion, too. Your drug of choice gives you a break from your habitual thinking. The addiction is actually to a clear mind, not the thing you mistakenly associate with giving you the feeling of a clear mind.)

There's nothing foolish about doing more of what you love to do; I just want you to understand the behind-the-scenes details a little better. Because if I believed it was the book or the floor or the collating, I'd feel pretty bad when writer's block crept up.

Yesterday, when I woke up wanting nothing at all to do with spreading this knowledge to the world—when I watched the neighbor girl get into her car dressed for her job at Applebee's and felt envious of her less cerebral, more physically active, more social career and wanted to trade places with her—it didn't matter.

That temporary blip didn't lead to a crisis because I knew the only things that had changed were my ever-changing level of consciousness and the extent to which I took my thoughts seriously.

If I believed my carpet party was responsible for that feeling I had, I'd feel pretty bad when I didn't have a free hour to roll around in my book. You would too, when you couldn't create your art or watch your movies.

And if I believed that my temporary discontent yesterday morning meant I needed to look for a new line of work, then I might be waiting tables now and you'd be reading something else.

When we understand how it really works, it doesn't have to be that way for either of us.

37.

WHOSE OPINION DO YOU TRUST?

"There is an enormous difference between finding your own inner wisdom and adopting someone else's beliefs."
—Sydney Banks in The Missing Link

Whose opinion do you trust?

When all of those outside opinions are screaming in your head, which one is loudest? Which carries the most weight?

The voice that sounds most assertive or confident?

The deepest one? The oldest one? The most religious or least religious one?

The one that comes from the person with the most life experience? The most college degrees? The most money?

The one that sounds like your parents? (You're wired to believe that one.)

The voice of the person most important to you? The one you most want to impress?

The opinion that tells you what you want to hear? Or maybe it's the one that confirms your biggest fears about yourself.

What about the voice that sounds like you? Why isn't that the clear and obvious winner? Or the "voice" that doesn't necessarily sound like a voice; the one that just knows, acts, and chooses without the mental hemming and hawing.

There are many reasons we don't always trust our own voice or the even the one that feels so clear. Many of those reasons have been discussed earlier in this book, but the *why* isn't all that important.

What matters is that you realize that no one could possibly know what's best for you better than you do.

They never have and they never will. It's time to stop letting them run the show.

38.

WHAT TO "DO" WITH YOUR SCARIEST THOUGHTS

"The hardest work of all is to do nothing."
—Proverb

I got up to change the baby's diaper last night and when I came back to bed, something seemed off about my husband. He seemed to be sleeping unusually still. I couldn't hear or see him breathing.

My mind immediately raced to what life would be like if he were dead.

Part of me was pretty sure he wasn't. That part said "He's been sleep deprived lately. He's just sleeping more soundly than usual."

Meanwhile, another part of my mind created some really horrific scenarios.

What if I reached over to touch him and he didn't wake up? What would I do with my two year old while the paramedics were trying to resuscitate him? Could I keep it together to not traumatize our kids any more than necessary?

I had a flash of clarity about how much I take our life together for granted. I was suddenly, 100% positive that I wanted our life to be exactly as it was. A flood of gratitude ensued, dimmed by a flood of terror that it could all end in an instant.

A minute later, the dog snored loudly and hubby flipped over. Alive!

I share this story because everyone's imagination spins horror stories from time to time.

The story itself is irrelevant. The nature of the horror, the frequency of the story, the emotion it stirs...all irrelevant.

The only thing that matters is what you do with it.

I was awake when this was all going on last night, but I could have just as easily been asleep. It could have just as easily been a dream. Dream or thought...what's the difference, really? He's alive. Either way, the awful outcome I dreamed up was a figment of my imagination.

So here's what I recommend doing with the horror stories your mind might spin: nothing.

Humans typically aren't fans of doing nothing. Here are a few of the things we tend to *do* with thoughts like these:

1. WE REPLAY THEM OVER AND OVER THROUGHOUT THE DAY

This requires effort. The nature of thought is such that it floats in and it floats out. To repeatedly return this thought to the front of your mind requires finding it and dragging it back. Or lavishing it with so much attention when it floats in that it never wants to leave.

2. WE TAKE THE THOUGHTS AS SIGNS

"It's a sign" is just another thought (and even if my thought was a sign...then what?) This hubby-is-dead thought was only a thought, like a nightmare is only a nightmare. Although it felt very real and scary, nothing changed in the world of form.

3. ASSUME ACTION IS REQUIRED

I could have demanded that my husband have his blood pressure checked and start eating more green vegetables. If you believe thought is meaningful and requires action, those steps make sense.

But if you get that thought doesn't require action any more than a nightmare does, what's the point?

Instead of any of the above, I chose to view those worst-case scenario moments as evidence that I am human, remind myself of the nature of thought, and do nothing.

That exact fear might come back. It may not. I have no idea. I might have the same nightmare tonight or I may never have it again. Your guess is as good as mine.

But when I get that thoughts aren't real...

And when I get that the nature of thought is that it floats in and it floats out...

There's simply nothing to "do."

CONVERSATIONS WITH CLIENTS

A:

"...You are thinking really sad thoughts and so you feel sad, it's that simple."

J:

"That makes sense to me—very clear. It's all about changing the way I think, then?"

A:

"I don't think of it as changing the way you think so much as relating to thought in a new way. Thought is arbitrary and meaningless. You give it meaning, but it has no inherent meaning. The only way thought has any power is when you pay attention to it and decide that you're going to believe one of those random thoughts that float your way.

"Also, your thinking is always changing, as you've no doubt noticed when you're sitting at work thinking about work, then lunch, then the weekend, then work again. It's an effortless, constant process.

If you met thoughts about your relationship, your future, and your worth with the same energy with which you meet thoughts about lunch or the weekend, those thoughts would arise and float away... no big deal.

"But of course you rarely do that—you (all of us) make things much harder by treating some thoughts (often the dramatic ones) as if they are true and putting stock in them. So, it's not about changing your thoughts so much as realizing that thought is only meaningful when you make it so."

J:

"...Last night I was supposed to get a call from him and I didn't. I got myself into an insecure little hole. I kept saying to myself, 'These are just thoughts. Try a new way of thinking.' I'm realizing it takes practice and patience because I had a hard time finding a new way of thinking!"

A:

"It can be near impossible to 'find a new way of thinking,' especially when you are feeling insecure already. Maybe rather than lack of practice it's just that changing your thoughts is not always possible.

"Instead of trying to think differently and then taking that new, happier thinking as truth, it helps to realize you're making it all up anyway. Yes, happier stories feel better than unhappy stories, but they are all just subjective thought-stories in the end.

"It's a ton of work to try to control your thinking and, in my experience, it rarely works as well or for as long as you'd like. It's much easier and seems to make more sense to just let it float along, knowing that new, different thought will be along shortly."

J:

"Ah, just let it float...! That feels so much better than trying to force positive thoughts!"

39.

PLAYING THE GAME:
A SHORT STORY ABOUT
WILLOW AND BUDDHA

"Fortunately, once you see what you really are, beyond any doubt, the identity crisis collapses and laughter and great relief ensues."
—*From The Lazy Man's Way to Enlightenment by David Bhodan*

My girl Willow has the most active imagination of anyone I've ever met. She's three, by the way.

She will make up scenarios with details that would blow your mind. I have no clue where she gets this stuff.

She's not only great at crafting stories, she also has the incredible ability to set aside reality and dive into her tales as if they were absolutely true.

This morning she was on my bed; Buddha, our Zen-like, seven pound Yorkie was lying on the floor.

I asked Willow to jump off the bed and follow me downstairs for breakfast. She looked down at Buddha and in a very dramatic, damsel-in-distress voice, said "But I'm scared of Buddha, she's going to get me! *Noooo*, Buddha, *nooo!*"

(Buddha, not amused, looked at me as if to say, "This again? Am I supposed to growl and nip at her feet or can I go back to sleep?")

I suggested to Willow that she hop in her hot air balloon and float over Buddha to get downstairs safely. (She often travels by hot air balloon.) Then I went downstairs and left her to figure it out.

Five minutes later, I was downstairs and Willow wasn't. She was crying on the bed.

"Come down!"

"I can't, I'm afraid of Buddha!" she cried, sounding honestly afraid.

She wasn't playing anymore. Or, more accurately, she forgot she was playing. She made up a story in her head and was so immersed in it that she forgot she invented it.

I went up to get her. Her face was soaked with real tears and she looked terrified. Of a sleepy seven pound dog named Buddha.

I reminded her that she was only playing a game where she *pretended* to be afraid of Buddha. That she wasn't really afraid. After a few moments, her face lit up and a huge smile appeared.

I said, "You forgot that you were playing a make believe game, didn't you?" She laughed and said, "I'm silly!"

She is silly, but she's also a lot like you and me. She gets so wrapped up in her own thinking that she forgets she's the one who invented it.

Adult Willows lose sleep over not living up to some beauty or brains standard, forgetting that they created their own false standards years ago.

Or they believe the voice that says "The neighbors don't like you," "You made a mistake," or "A glass of wine will fix that." They forget that there is no correlation between a thought floating into awareness and that thought being true. Just like my Willow, adult Willows lose themselves in the story.

Those are person-level examples of buying into the illusion of thought—but all of life is an illusion in a similar way.

We are connected to every living thing, but we forget. I believe we're playing a game where we inhabit human bodies and brains that make it appear as if we're separate. Different sexes, different skin colors, different beliefs...as if any of that matters. Believing there is a distinct you, me, us, and them.

We forget that the separation is all just part of the illusion. We forget that when the personal thinking and identification with "me" drops away, we're all exactly the same.

Playing make believe is fun, especially when you temporarily forget you're playing a game.

Slowly waking up to the game is fun too.

She made up a story in her head and was so immersed in it she forgot she invented it.

Amy Johnson

40.

SPINNING THROUGH OUTER SPACE

"You are sitting on a planet spinning through outer space."
—Michael Singer in The Untethered Soul:
The Journey Beyond Yourself

In his book *The Untethered Soul*, Michael Singer says something so obviously simple and true that it's been messing with my head ever since. (Truth is astonishingly simple, always.)

He says we're sitting on a planet spinning through outer space.

Oh, yeah! I forgot. Did you?

I see people get stuck in their psychology all the time. It's not their fault—your view of the world is filtered through your mind, and your mind tries its hardest to convince you that what it thinks is right.

But while our psychology creates our *experience* of life, *it's not life.* There is a much bigger truth out there than "The other kids made fun of me," "My mom was mean," "I'm insecure/broke/sick," or "I'm addicted to alcohol." There is much more that is fundamentally *you* than those little aspects of your personal psychology.

You're sitting on a planet spinning through outer space.

Those things happened in your past and you had reactions to them. And then they stopped happening. Did your reactions to them stop? Or do you keep them alive by dragging them back into your current consciousness?

You're sitting on a planet spinning through outer space.

But *you don't understand,* I hear you thinking. *This really affected me. I haven't been the same since. I can't let go. I can't forgive. I can't trust again, even though I want to.*

You can't? You're sitting on a planet spinning through outer space. You're a speck in the incredible universe. Isn't it worth a shot?

Isn't it worth letting down your guard, admitting that maybe everything you believe is wrong, opening up?

You're just sitting on a planet spinning through outer space. For now, anyway. Someday your body will die and "you" won't be "sitting" anywhere anymore.

This spinning through outer space business does something big for me. It makes me want to say screw it to all the holding on and being right and just live full out while I can because, honestly, why not?

I hope it does something similar for you.

41.

WHAT TO DO WITH THE PAIN

This essay was written on December 17, 2012, 3 days after 28 people were tragically killed at Sandy Hook Elementary School.

"When I was a boy and I would see scary things in the news, my mother would say to me, 'Look for the helpers. You will always find people who are helping.'"
—*Mister Rogers*

When our thoughts drift to—and fixate on—horrible events in the world, we hurt.

If you pay attention, you'll notice that your thoughts will also drift *away* from those thoughts, and you don't hurt in those moments. Even in the midst of unspeakable pain, thoughts part like the clouds and the sun peeks out. Your peace of mind shines through for a minute or two before the clouds roll back through.

Those moments of peace are okay. They are part of the design.

It's okay to not hurt, even when others are hurting.

Your pain doesn't change what happened. It doesn't take away the pain of parents whose children are gone. It doesn't prevent tragedy from happening again.

It just means that one more person is in pain—you.

Feel what you feel when you feel it. But also remember—you will always feel your thinking and your thinking isn't cemented in place. It is fluid, always floating in and out like the clouds.

It's not honorable or helpful to endlessly watch the news coverage, stare at pictures of grieving parents, or incessantly recite the names of deceased children. It's fine if you want to do that, but it's not *noble* or *helpful* to do so.

Personally, I find that having those images accessible in my mind only causes me to hurt much more. It doesn't take the pain away from anyone else. It doesn't prevent future tragedy. It only spreads and prolongs the hurt.

When I feel the temptation to put myself in those parents' shoes and go deeply into what they must be feeling, I attempt to pull back from those thoughts, send them a small prayer for peace, and spread a bit of love to the people around me instead.

We were all born happy and at peace. We restore that peaceful default by focusing on the love and peace all around us, *not* by focusing on where and when and how it sometimes goes horribly wrong.

I'm not talking about denying anything. I'm only saying that choosing to use pain as a reason to spread love makes a lot more sense than choosing to sit in pain.

I know it's idealistic and it might feel like "not enough," but we really do change the world starting with ourselves and the people around us. The world doesn't change via laws or legislation or debates. It changes when you make absolutely sure that your children understand their true nature.

Make sure they know that no matter how bad things feel, they are only feeling their thoughts and that thoughts can change in an instant.

Teach them that their true nature is infinite love and peace of mind and that the clouds will part if they allow them to. It's never, ever as bad as their thinking would have them believe.

And if you don't have children of your own, please share this with someone else's children. They are going to need to hear it more than once, with a variety of words and in a variety of voices, so let's just keep saying it.

42.

HOW MUCH PLEASURE
WILL YOU ALLOW?

"Life is to be enjoyed, not endured."
—*Gordon B. Hinckley*

"Find ecstasy in life; the mere sense of living is joy enough."
—*Emily Dickenson*

Sometimes a quote just speaks to you. This is one of those for me.

"When you die, God and the Angels will hold you accountable for all the pleasures you were allowed in life that you denied yourself."
—Roger Housden

I've read this over and over. Each time, I sound like Meg Ryan in that famous diner scene.

Yes. YES. Yes. I *so* believe *this* is the point of it all.

Not the "hold you accountable" part....well, not in any kind of literal way that has anything at all to do with punishment or shame or "you were wrong."

But that...yes...it is *supposed to be* pleasure-filled.

Pleasure-*filled*. Not "so so" with spikes of pleasure here and there.

Not work-filled with pleasure on the weekends, and not a lot of hard work for a few decades so you can experience pleasure later.

Pleasure-*filled*.

Given that, aren't you grateful that pleasure comes from within? If pleasure came from what you chose to do with your life or what the people around you chose to do with their lives, pleasure would be hard to come by. It would be inconsistent and random and never quite within reach.

A pleasure-filled life would be almost impossible, don't you think?

Thank God that's not the case.

CONVERSATIONS WITH CLIENTS

B:

"Last night came and I didn't want to do anything. I fell into another little trap last night and yesterday."

A:

"When you say you didn't want to do anything, do you mean you didn't want to do any of the things your mind said you *should* want to do? I mean, you must have wanted to do *something*, right? Sleep, eat, stare at your goldfish...something? I'm guessing you mean you didn't want to do any of the 'right' things—but tell me where I'm wrong.

"When days and nights come when you don't want to do any mind-approved activities, see if you can try not to think of those as 'traps.' There are many times when your natural preferences are not in line with what your mind has decided you *should* do in order to be good enough. But that's okay because the good news is, *your mind is wrong*. You don't actually need to run all over Manhattan doing all the 'right' things to be good enough. You don't have to do anything at all."

B:

"That makes sense, it really does. It doesn't feel true in the moment but I *know* it's true. Last night though, it really did feel like there was *nothing* I wanted to do."

A:

"Is it okay to do nothing? Isn't it okay to do nothing once in a while?"

B:

"Why do I keep forgetting that? It is okay!"

சாக்ஜ

B:

"So I know we just covered this the other day but I'm having a tough time with it again. I'm getting so bent out of shape over here because I really should go for a walk but I don't feel like it. I know I'm making it so much harder than it is. Again. Help?"

A:

"Why should you go for a walk?"

B:

"Because it's so nice outside."

A:

"So?"

B:

"Nice weather is rare these days so I feel like I should take advantage of it. I've also been too busy to walk much this month, and then I hurt my knee and couldn't walk for a while. Now my knee is better so I feel like I should fit in a quick one, at least."

A:

"Sorry...*why* should you go for a walk?

"I'm not seeing how the weather or a healthy knee translates into 'I should go for a walk.' It's nice outside my house, too, and my knees feel great, and yet *I* shouldn't go for a walk. Why should you?"

B:

"Umm... I guess I feel like I ought to do something productive with my time. I should get the walk in so that I can relax later if I want to."

A:

"You can relax any time you want, whether you've walked or not. Who decided a walk is productive?"

B:

"I decided it! And I know I could relax either way, but I know me and I probably won't. If I do, I won't truly relax because I'll be thinking I should have gone on that walk! Urg...I make things so hard on myself."

A:

"You and everyone else I know; you're in good company. But honestly, it's your choice, B. You invented the rule that a walk is more productive than anything else you might choose, and you're the only one enforcing it. If you decide someday that playing or resting or reading is the most productive thing you could do, that will be an option too.

"You can live by any rules you want, I just want you to see that you're the sole rule maker and the lone rule police."

B:

"I guess I do know that. It definitely doesn't feel like I've made up my own rules though—they feel like the obvious truth with a capital T. But I guess I do know that they started with me."

A:

"I hear you, B. My thoughts feel true too, especially the strict ones and the ones that 'society' and the lady next door would agree with. Still, they aren't truth with a capital T. They are story with a capital S."

B:

"I know. One last question for you...what do you base *your* decisions on? If I don't base my actions on what my thoughts tell me to do, then what should I base them on? How will I ever really know what to do?"

A:

"I'm not sure there is one catch-all guiding principle but one that occurs to me is...pleasure? What if you base your decisions on what brings you pleasure? On what feels delicious in the moment?

"As far as I can tell from watching Willow, Miller, and any other kid before they begin to take their thinking seriously, the only guiding principle that governs their behavior is 'Is it fun?' Or the related, 'Do I want to?'

"So, B...setting all else aside, ignoring the fact that 'I should go for a walk' *feels* like truth right now, not making the beautiful weather or your happy knee mean anything in particular...do you *want to* go for a walk?"

B:

"No. I want to relax. I want to take a nap, actually."

A:

"Sweet dreams."

43.

BEHIND THE VEIL

"You are perfect exactly as you are. With all your flaws and problems, there's no need to change anything. All you need to change is the thought that you aren't good enough."
—Jermaine Lamarr Cole (J. Cole)

You are perfect. There is nothing wrong with you.

As I promised in the introduction, you didn't just read a self-help book; in fact, "self-help" itself is a massive misnomer. The only help I hope to provide is helping you to remember what the deepest part of you never forgot.

Remember that when your perfection and peace of mind are not obvious, they are only momentarily veiled by personal thinking.

Remember that personal thinking is highly subjective. Arbitrary, even. That everything you see "out in the world" is actually created within you. There is no "out there" in the absence of your own creative thinking.

Remember that there is nothing you have to do. There are no steps or rules and there's nothing you need to improve upon.

Remember that you already are that which you are seeking. Your true nature is connection and wellness, and that returning there is more an undoing than a doing. Going back to your natural state only requires getting out of the way.

Remember that whatever condition or circumstance you think will make you happy will not, actually. Conditions and circumstances don't create happiness.

Remember that you are as resilient as any young child. You are naturally and effortlessly bounced back to your wellbeing the instant you stop attaching to personal thought.

Remember that wanting what you have means that all of your wishes instantly come true.

Remember that a clear, blank, "dumb" mind—a mind that you're willing to change at any time—is a beautiful thing.

Remember that helping others and healing the world starts with understanding your true nature and knowing that, as bad as things might seem, separation and pain are illusory.

Remember that bad moods and bad days are only feedback about your current thinking, nothing more. Practice leaning into them and even welcoming them, and see how comfortable they become.

Remember that your past can change in an instant. Forgiving and viewing your past through fresh thought rewrites history.

Remember that people aren't mean, they are insecure or hurting. And when you and another person come together as a team, your relationship is reborn.

Remember that you don't have to figure it all out. It's already figured out.

Remember that pleasure is the point, you're spinning on a planet in outer space, and you're making up the rules of the game as you go and then forgetting that you made them up.

And remember that you don't need to "remember" any of this; it is built into who you are. No Post-it notes, no memorization. No mantras or repetition, unless you enjoy those things—and then only do them for the fun of it.

When you take your thinking less seriously, the veil shifts and perfection and peace of mind are right there waiting for you.

That is the only self-help there is.

"The top 10 things people claim to have taken for granted when they were alive:

10. How important they were to so many.
9. How easy life was when they stopped struggling.
8. That all of their prayers and thoughts were heard.
7. That there really were no coincidences.
6. How far ripples of their kindness actually spread.
5. What really was important: happiness, friends, love.
4. That any and all of their dreams could have come true.
3. How good looking and fun they always were.
2. How much guidance they received, whenever
they asked for help.
1. That God was alive in everything, including themselves.

As expressed by the recently departed, fresh after their life-review on the big, BIG screen.

Ah-so,
The Universe"

—The Universe (via Mike Dooley, www.tut.com)

Gratitude

Believe it or not, this is by far the most difficult part of this book for me to write.

I tend to get quite caught up in my head, thinking of all the people who have supported me in countless ways, lamenting the lack of space and the futility of words in thanking each of them.

So. Much. Thinking.

So I whittle the list way down and vow to keep it relatively simple. I'm letting my fingers move along the keyboard with as little thinking as possible. Here goes.

I feel loads of gratitude for the few thousand people who faithfully read my weekly newsletter and blog each week, and especially for the handful of you who routinely email me to agree, disagree, praise, or question what I write about. Those everyday exchanges are incredibly encouraging. Sending your experiences of life into the interwebs and wondering with who or what they might be colliding can be pretty humbling; you all show me that my thoughts actually are reaching human life and that they make a difference. Specifically (well, as specific as you can get with first names only), I'd like to thank Jacquellyn, Doug, Patrick, Michaela, Luc, Jessica, and Marion for your consistent notes of encouragement and challenge. You are the unofficial, first draft editors of this book (especially you, Jacq!). I'd also like to thank Gita for your creative metaphors and invented words.

Speaking of editors, I owe a universe of thanks to Lynn Hess, the best editor and idea-bouncer-off-er I could have ever asked for on this project. Your deep understanding of these ideas and your impeccable proofing skills made this book far better than it would have otherwise been. What's really crazy is that you were the first person to utter the phrase "Three Principles" to me. You weren't sure what the three principles actually were (one was Thought, but what were the other two?), but you knew enough to hang out in their vicinity. Smart girl. Thank you a million times for everything.

Janette Gregson, your unique, creative talents have also made this book far better than it otherwise would have been. As soon as I saw your art journals I knew they were something special and that knowing is reconfirmed each time I see another piece of yours. Thank you so much for believing in what this book is about and trusting your gut to work on this project even when I was a complete stranger.

Without my courageous and oh-so-human clients, I'd have far less to write about. Thank you for trusting me to point you in the right direction and for not hanging up the phone when I tell you that you might be wrong about everything you think you know. You are incredibly inspiring.

I'd like to express my gratitude for my official and mostly unofficial mentors, whose wisdom is truly what this book is built upon. I've personally worked with some of you and others of you have no idea who I am but your books, videos, interviews, and programs have significantly added to my understanding of life. Thank you to Michael Neill, Dicken Bettinger, Sydney Banks, Bill Pettit, Mara Gleason, Linda Pransky, George Pransky, Tom Shadyac, Rudi Kennard, Jenny Kennard, David Bhodan, and Michael Singer...to name only a few.

Finally, thank you to my entire family, especially my mom (the best mom, friend, and Dobby around), my awesome sisters, and my in-laws.

There are seriously are no words to express my gratitude for my husband. You hold everything together and make our amazing life possible, Ora. You are our rock.

And thank you to Willow and Miller for being constant living examples of our natural state. You are wise, hilarious, kind little souls who make life fun and remind us that all is well. When my blog readers refer to you as "the world's youngest life coaches," as they very often do, nothing makes me more proud. The two of you are showing others how to return to their true nature by simply being exactly who you are. I am blessed to get to chase you around for the next couple decades.

Done! Thank you, thank you, thank you.

Resources

Below are some of my all-time favorite books and websites for learning more about the ideas I've written about. Many of these resources were either mentioned in, or greatly inspired, this book.

Books:

The Lazy Man's Way to Enlightenment: What You're Looking For Is What Is Looking by David A. Bhodan

The Untethered Soul: The Journey Beyond Yourself by Michael Singer

You Can Be Happy No Matter What: Five Principles for Keeping Life in Perspective by Richard Carlson

The Inside-Out Revolution: The Only Thing You Need to Know to Change Your Life Forever by Michael Neill

Clarity: Clear Mind, Better Performance, Bigger Results by Jamie Smart

The Relationship Handbook by George Pransky

The Enlightened Gardner: A Novel by Sydney Banks

The Enlightened Gardner Revisited by Sydney Banks

Second Chance by Sydney Banks

The Missing Link: Reflections on Philosophy and Spirit by Sydney Banks

Our True Identity...Three Principles by Elsie Spittle

Websites:

Three Principles Movies: www.threeprinciplesmovies.com

> This is an amazing site full of totally free videos about the Three Principles understanding.

Three Principles Global Community: www.3PGC.com

> The Three Principles Global Community is a non-profit organization that is committed to bringing an understanding of The Three Principles to people throughout the world.

If You Want More...

If you'd like additional support in deepening your understanding of your innate wellbeing, I'd love to help. Here are just a few of the ways I can support you in applying this understanding to your own life.

PERSONAL COACHING

Work one-on-one with me as your personal coach. Personal coaching consists primarily of regular telephone calls or back-and-forth email correspondence—whichever method best fits your life. This is the best way to deepen your grounding in the ideas discussed here so that your experience of life becomes infinitely easier and more peaceful. To learn more about personal coaching visit www.DrAmyJohnson.com/coaching.

PUBLIC SPEAKING

I speak to groups about creativity, resiliency and bouncing back, effortless relationships, and virtually any topic that helps people live a better life. I love to tailor talks or presentations to your particular group or purpose. Contact me at Amy@DrAmyJohnson.com to bring me into your organization.

GET MY FREE EBOOK AND STAY IN TOUCH

For even more support getting out of your own way, you can download my free eBook, *15 Ways You're Blocking Your Own Happiness. And 15 Things to Do Instead* at www.DrAmyJohnson.com. When you sign up there, you'll also receive free weekly articles and updates anytime I offer a new coaching opportunity, class, or free product.

About the Author

Dr. Amy Johnson is a master certified life coach, social psychologist, and public speaker.

She has taught university-level psychology, consulted on several high-profile court cases, spoken to audiences around the country about success and happiness, and sailed completely around the globe.

Amy works with clients all over the world via telephone and online coaching programs. If you're interested in learning more about the inside-out nature of life and getting out of your own way so that you can have a more peaceful experience on this planet, she can help.

Since her first book, *Modern Enlightenment: Psychological, Spiritual, and Practical Ideas for a Better Life*, was published in 2012, she has been a regular featured expert on *The Steve Harvey Show* and *Oprah. com*, as well as in *The Wall Street Journal* and *Self Magazine*.

Amy is also the wife of a Green Bay Packer fanatic and mommy to two wise-beyond-their-years toddlers. She's into coffee, world travel, documentaries, library books, and sleeping through the night.

Please sign up at www.DrAmyJohnson.com to stay up to date on Amy's new essays, books, and appearances.

Made in the USA
Lexington, KY
17 July 2015